The Pastor's Personal Friendships

Conflicts, Boundaries, and Benefits

David B. Simmons

Doctor of Ministry
Thesis Project

Gordon-Conwell Theological Seminary

The Pastor's Personal Friendships:
Conflicts Boundaries, and Benefits

Originally submitted to
Gordon-Conwell Theological Seminary

In Partial Fulfillment of the Degree Requirements for
Doctor of Ministry

May 2014

This book is dedicated to my father

Bobby J. Simmons
(1942-2007)

who encouraged me in all my educational pursuits.

He would be proud.

Contents

Acknowledgements

The document before you is a labor of love that has been stirring in me for more than four years. Its completion comes with a cost, given that the hours and mental toil are far more than can be calculated. But despite the costs, the joys have far exceeded the pain. However, I realize that in the achievement of this task, my joy often comes at the cost and sacrifice of others. And to those wonderful people in my life, I offer my deepest gratitude.

I first thank the congregations of Temple Baptist Church in Newport News, Virginia, and Locust Lane Chapel in Harrisburg, Pennsylvania. I had the privilege of pastoring both of these congregations during the time I pursued my doctoral studies. It was during these pastorates that I wrestled with the balance between being a pastor and being a friend. I also express great appreciation for their financial support, which was significant in making this project possible. How grateful I am to them for investing in me, even though the benefits of that investment would likely bear fruit in other places and in another time.

To the ten pastors who participated in this study, I express my appreciation for your willingness to think aloud with me about this oft overlooked subject. I was grateful to sit at the feet of your wisdom. I was humbled and encouraged to hear you express openly the victories and defeats of ministry and how your friends shared your unique journeys. Any benefit to what is found in these pages is owed to your insights. May God continue to bless you in your respective ministries and grant you great friendships.

To Dr. Ken Swetland, you truly embody the word "mentor." Your sage advice and encouragement were exactly what I needed at each critical step along the way. I cherish your wisdom and deeply value your patience. I am convinced you continue to delay retirement just to see me graduate! I hope this helps. To Dr. David Horn, Dr. David Currie, and the D.Min. staff of Gordon Conwell, I extend my gratitude for each part you have contributed to my education and this project. I am also grateful to my many colleagues at Hershey Medical Center who have cheered me on to the finish line.

To my mother, Patsy, and brother, Brandon, I am so grateful that you agreed to read and edit my work. It was wonderful to know that if no one ever decided to read this project all the way through, at least I had an audience of two!

Finally, to my beautiful wife, Tara, and my amazing children, Connor, Alex, and Lillie, I thank you for all the many weekends and evenings you sacrificed so I could devote myself to this project. Throughout this project, I stayed committed to the notion that it is never wise for the pastor's spouse to bear the full weight of "friend." Yet, after all I have imagined about what a friend is, I have become fully aware that you, Tara, are without a doubt my best friend. You know my thoughts before I think them, challenge me when I need challenged, and console me when I am in need. I know that we both long for robust friendships in our lives, but in the absence of that, I am ever grateful to have you as my friend and so much more.

David Simmons
March 30, 2014

Introduction

"You are the tool."

These were the slow and deliberate words graced to me by a beloved and cherished mentor as he spoke gently into the doubts surrounding my pastoral identity. These are words that have since changed the way I think of myself as pastor, leader, and caregiver. Physicians have their stethoscopes, carpenters have their plumb lines, and artists have their canvases. But for pastors, it is their own being that presses into the lives of those they serve. Yes, we have our faith, our theology, our Scriptures, and our intimate relationship with God, but if those deeply influential forces do not shape us into loving and nurturing human beings that positively connect to the ones we serve, we are but "a resounding gong or a clanging symbol."

As I have reflected on these wise words and have allowed them to shape my thinking, I have grown to appreciate something else about them. Not only is the pastor's being the tool through which God works in others, but it is through relationships that the pastor-as-tool begins to make a difference. Without relationships, the pastor is but a futile instrument. One might attempt to offer up other attractive alternatives, like a good sermon or a thoughtful insight or a three point plan, but none of those have effectual sway until those ideas are transmitted through genuine and transformative relationship. Like colorful inks sitting idly before a barren canvas, none are made good until taken into the hands of the Grand Artist, mixed into the right hues and shades, and then pressed into the textured possibility of the canvas.

If the church is called to shape the world, pastors are God's tools to His church. To make strides in this considerable task, each pastor bears the burden of continual self-awareness and relational mindfulness. The pastor must be skilled in both the world of being and the world of relating. Who am I? And who am I in relationship to others? How does the development of who I am shape the way I influence others? The effective pastor continually mulls over these questions, monitoring the inward forces and the relational connections that give ministry its shape. A pastor is always thinking about his[1] relationships. A pastor is

---

[1] Regarding the use of gender specific pronouns, I have found the constant use of "he or she" and "his and her" language to produce the most awkward of sentences. But I also realize that to use one gender pronoun and not another will leave one wondering if I have

continually examining how she connects with others, for it is through relationships that the Spirit forms and transforms.

Given the importance of pastoral relationships, the pastor-in-training is often invited to reflect on the array of relationships that the pastor will encounter. The hope is that future clergy will be shaped into effective relational beings. Yet despite the wide range of relational training, the one relationship that is least considered is the pastor's friendships. Pastors may become experts in leading their elders or in counseling the hurting or comforting the grieving, but pastors are rarely encouraged to think about their friendships. Perhaps because friendships are such pleasurable experiences, we find little need to consider them. After all, it is the difficult relationships that are our priority. Friendships are a concern of one's personal life, not their professional life. Why devote much attention to them?

The project before you is an attempt to direct the pastor's attention to the impact of this much overlooked, but deeply influential relationship. Friendships are not innocuous relationships outside the purview of the pastor's concern. They are an integrated component of many a pastoral relationship. Many of the key pastoral relationships will develop some characteristics of friendship. How will that affect the relationship? What should a pastor now be aware of? It is not a question of whether a pastor will have friends. The question is whether or not the pastor will engage those friendships with full awareness of their effect on his or her ministry.

Not only is one's understanding of friendship a factor in the complexities of pastoral relationships, but the pastor's personal friendships are a key component of healthy self-care strategy. This will be a key component of this project. I argue throughout that the pastor's personal friendships ought to be a key figure in the pastor's personal support team. Because personal friendships are less formal than the other more professional relationships of ministry, they are often considered to be less essential in the formation of a pastoral support system.

This project seeks to reverse that assumption. Unlike the pastor's professional relationships which touch primarily on the professional needs of ministry, the pastor's friendships reach into the heart of the pastor's

---

been sensitive to the presence of the other gender in ministry. Another may wonder if the use of the feminine pronoun is my effort at advancing an agenda. Being that there is no good answer, I have chosen to allow the structure of the sentence to prevail over gender sensitivity issues. When "he or she" flows well, I will use more inclusive language. When it becomes awkward, I will chose a single pronoun and alternate between the male and female pronouns. I offer my apologies ahead of time for any stumbling block this causes to the reader.

private life.[2] Like professional relationships, friendships provide a place to unload the burdens of pastoral ministry. Yet friendship provides something professional relationships cannot. Friendship enables the pastor to escape his role and the expectations, stress, and busyness that accompany it.

This project also examines another aspect of the pastor's friendships, namely that friendships do not come easily for the pastor. Complexities unique to the profession abound. How does a pastor find time to nurture her friendships when she is plagued by high demands and a busy schedule? If a pastor develops close friendships within the congregation, how safe is it to develop these kinds of personal friendships? Traditionally speaking, the greater the friendship, the greater the pastor can "be himself." Yet how can a pastor express vulnerable with a congregational friend who may have high view of the pastoral role? What does this do to the professional and ministry relationship a pastor has with the people she calls friends? Can the friend inside the church be depended upon to sustain the pastor during tough times, or will their expectations of their pastor get in the way of the friendship? Once one begins to see the layers of complexity involved with pastors and their friendships, it becomes understandable why, according to the 1991 Fuller Institute of Church Growth survey of pastors, 70 percent of pastors reported having no close friend.[3]

Through the research and examination conducted in this project, I will seek an answer to the question, who can be the pastor's friend? Beginning in Chapter One, I will lay out a picture of the particular complexities a pastor faces in congregational ministry today. We will look at contemporary pastoral life, its excruciating demands, and the importance of including the pastor's personal friendships as a part of his or her personal support system.

Chapter Two will ask the question, what is friendship? I will examine how friendships are formed, what good they provide, and what needs they fulfill in a person. A cursory look at the attitudes of philosophers and thinkers throughout history as well as the sociologists of our day will help us track the evolving nature of friendships over time and most importantly where friendships stand today.

Once the nature and importance of friendships are established, I will, in Chapter Three, examine the thorny and complicated issue of friendships within the church. Should a pastor have friends inside the

---

2 Raymond E. Pahl, *On Friendship* (Walden, MA: Polity Press, 2000), 13.

3 "1991 Survey of Pastors," Fuller Church Growth Institute, as quoted in H. B. London and Neil B. Wiseman, *Pastors at Greater Risk* (Ventura, CA: Gospel Light, 2003) 264.

church? What are the benefits of making congregational friends, and what pitfalls or compromises potentially negate the benefits of those friendships? Can a pastor be friend *and* counselor? Friend *and* leader? Friend *and* shepherd?

Then, in Chapter Four, I will take us beyond the local congregation to the extended world of the pastor to ask, where can a pastor go and what can a pastor do to cultivate friendships outside the church? Is friendship with fellow pastors the answer to the pastor's friendship needs? Are there friendship resources outside the congregation the pastor has not considered?

Finally, in Chapter Five, I will offer some final recommendations that will guide the pastor towards a fruitful friendship life. My ultimate aim is to encourage pastors to become intentional about seeking out and developing close friendships and to lean upon these friends to provide personal support to his or her well-being. My hope is that pastors will take time to settle into the replenishing and peaceful world of friendship and draw out all the meaning it has for the pastor's well-being and effectiveness in ministry. I pray that that the research, reflections, and insights provided in these pages brings honor to the work of serious-minded pastors who bear the great task of standing before the church as God's tool of care and influence. May this work contribute to the most effective use of that tool.

CHAPTER I

The Challenges of Contemporary Pastoral Life

For the Christian believer, Jesus Christ is the hope of the world. The Christian faith, rooted in the person and work of Christ and the power of the Holy Spirit in the world, offers a new and alternative, life-giving kingdom that exists "on earth as it is in heaven."[1] It presents a confident, future hope rooted in an objective reality that will one day be known and experienced.[2] The hope of this new kingdom gives us a vision of community that far exceeds anything human beings have ever known.[3] It is this alternative life of peace and grace that the church is called to model before an anxious world. The church is called to this task as it bears the image of God in the world and engages the world as Christ's Body. As the Body of Christ, the church stands in the world of violence, bitterness, and strife to offer peace, forgiveness, and mercies as the source of deliverance in the world.

While this may be the calling of the church, the reality is that the anxiety of the world seems to have settled in the church. Sanctuaries that once offered refuge against the ills of the world are now plagued with a growing and troubling uncertainty. In the chaos of contemporary life, the church is in a struggle for its own identity. Can it trust that Christ is the hope of the world and model peace before an anxious world? Or does the church have to act, to beat the world at its own power games, and to match the world's strategies with its own counter-attack? Everything is changing, and the church is struggling in a period of uncertainty, battling within its own ranks about how to be today's church in today's world.

Within the doors of today's church, its key caretaker–the pastor–is struggling to manage. The anxieties of the church are taking its toll on the pastor. The complexities of the pastorate are now being brought to light by staggering numbers of burnout, depression and suicide, family strife and divorce, and unprecedented levels of forced terminations. The public scandals of child sexual abuse and moral failures add to the declining reputation of today's clergy. Resembling more a soldier entering the field

---

[1] Matthew 6:10. Unless otherwise noted, all Bible references are from *The New International Version* (NIV).

[2] Jeremiah 29:11; Romans 8:24-25; Revelation 21:1-6

[3] Acts 2:42-47

of battle than a collared professional gracing the halls of a solemn sanctuary, the contemporary pastor engages in a brazen battle against spiritual, cultural, personal and ecclesiastical challenges unrivaled in recent decades.

So much has changed in a short time. The church has lost its place of prominence in the culture, and the pressure is growing for pastors to respond with staggering strength and insight. As pastors fail to meet these ever rising expectations, congregational harmony turns into ecclesiastical conflict. This conflict, when unresolved and unabated, preys upon the pastor's spiritual and physical strength. Slowly, disappointments begin to outweigh successes, expectations overwhelm the pastor's capabilities, and time demands outlast the pastor's energies. It is then that pastors and their families, either by force or by choice, slink away wounded and broken, often troubled in the conflict they feel between their absence of vitality and the conviction of their calling.

A number of studies[4] have revealed a distressing story. Studies reveal that just under half of all pastors have experienced burnout or depression to the degree that they felt they needed to take a leave of absence.[5] Twenty one percent have sought help for depression through medication or professional counseling[6] with the same number stating that anxiety and depression has recently affected their work.[7] One study shows that nearly a quarter of all pastors have been forced out of their congregations.[8] Even more troubling is that one in five clergy admits to having had an affair while in ministry, while a full third admit to "inappropriate sexual behavior" with someone in the church.[9] As one *New York Times* article stated, "In the last decade, [pastors'] use of

---

[4] For the statistics that follow, it was difficult to ascertain in all cases the accuracy of the surveys. Some have raised questions about the quality of some oft-quoted studies. When possible, I have sought to find a verifying source to add credibility to these numbers.

[5] H. B. London Jr. and Neil B. Wiseman, *Pastors at Greater Risk*, (Ventura, CA: Regal Books, 2003), 172.

[6] "Pastoral Ministries 2009 Survey," (Colorado Springs: Focus on the Family, 2009): 8, accessed January 27, 2011, http://fergusonconsultinggroup.com/images/Pastoral_Survey_ 2009.pdf.

[7] "Pulpit and Pew National Survey of Pastoral Leaders" (Pulpit & Pew, 2001), accessed March 17, 2013, http://www.thearda.com/Archive/Files/Codebooks/ CLERGY01_CB.asp.

[8] G. Lloyd Rediger, *Clergy Killers* (Louisville, KY: Westminster John Knox Press, 1997), 7. This was recently confirmed by Focus on the Family whose survey of over 2,000 pastors asked, "Have you ever experienced a forced resignation/termination?" Twenty four percent responded "yes." ("Pastoral Ministries 2009 Survey," 5.)

[9] Rediger, *Clergy Killers*, 7.

antidepressants has risen, while their life expectancy has fallen," noting ominously, "Many would change jobs if they could."[10]

No pastor starts out in ministry wanting to feel this way. In fact, nine out of ten say they feel positively about being in ministry, and three of four wish strongly to remain in ministry.[11] Eighty seven percent affirm that they have a strong sense of God's call and 86 percent would choose the profession if they had to do it over again.[12] Simply put, pastors want to pastor. They stand ready at their posts. Yet, many a pastor struggles to develop the kind of healthy, balanced lifestyle that can propel him to the end of a lifetime of meaningful ministry.

How, then, do pastors survive? How do pastors who entered ministry with a prolific drive and energy avoid crashing on the rocks of stress and burnout? How do pastors tune their bodies, their ministries, their spirits, and their skills in such a way that will enable them to navigate effectively through the turbulence of troubled times and the difficult demands that accompany them?

Part of the answer lies in the pastor's personal support system. It is generally accepted in clergy circles that in order to develop and maintain strong personal and spiritual health, the pastor must surrounded herself with a protective and nurturing support system. This system has both solitary and relational dimensions to it. Solitary practices are necessary to nurture the pastor's soul and inspire spiritual strength for living out the call. Rest, exercise, learning, Sabbath practices, solitude, spiritual disciplines, reading, meditation, and cognitive restructuring, all bolster the inner life of the pastor. Alongside these solitary practices come a web of personal and professional relationships that are "vital to our personal wholeness and professional effectiveness."[13] These relationships are numerous and varied and include family members, denominational mentors, educators, pastoral colleagues, spiritual directors, counselors, and accountability partners. These relationships are "dependable sources of healing, defense, guidance, and prevention of abuse."[14]

In the midst of this web of supportive relationships is an often overlooked relationship that can stand as a source of strength and encouragement in the face of increasing challenges. That is the pastor's

---

[10] Vitello, Paul, "Taking a Break From the Lord's Work," *New York Times*, August 1, 2010, accessed August 30, 2010, http://www.nytimes.com/2010/08/02/nyregion/02burnout.html.

[11] Kevin Miller, "What Pastors are Saying," LeadershipJournal.net, December 5, 2001, accessed January 25, 2011, http://www.christianitytoday.com/le/currenttrendscolumns/leadershipweekly/cln11205.html.

[12] London and Wiseman, *Pastors at Greater Risk,* 62.

[13] Rediger, *Clergy Killers*, 147.

[14] Rediger, *Clergy Killers*, 147.

friendships. One of the goals of this project is to advocate for the importance of pastors friendships as a means of personal support for the pastor. The personal friend provides an outlet for escaping the challenges of the pastoral demands and finding replenishment in the comfort of an accepting relationship. Friendship provides the pastor with a personal confidant, a trusted listener, and judicious guide. Friendship supplies the pastor with recreation and enjoyment. Friendship offers the joy of a common interest. Friendship provides a safe place for the pastor to simply "be" instead of "do." Friendship offers the antidote to isolation and the solution to loneliness. Ultimately, friendship gives flesh and insight to what it means to be a "friend of God," a term Abraham embraced–a term all believers embrace–when our faith is credited as righteousness.[15] Simply put, a pastor needs good friends.

To gain further insight on the importance of friendships as a key component to a pastoral support system, we must first confront the situations and circumstances in contemporary life and culture that is driving the need for pastors to be well protected. The pastor navigates through vastly different waters than in times past. In the pages that follow, I will move us into the world in which the pastor now lives, looking closely at the contemporary challenges confronting the pastor, at the cultural and congregational influences shaping pastoral expectations.

The New Face of Pastoral Life

The pastoral milieu has changed. Pressures and expectations on the pastor now dwarf those of previous decades. Going back a century or more, the values within American culture were far more homogeneous and in harmony with the Judeo-Christian ethic. This provided a more stable society and a pattern of predictability for the pastor's life and work. The absence of television, movies, and other media meant that values designed to compete with the Judeo-Christian worldview were kept far away. A protestant centered public school system helped to promote a loyalty to the Judeo-Christian values taught in the churches. Greater stability in family life meant lower divorce rates and more self-reliant families.

The local church served as the epicenter of a town's social life. Sabbath laws were observed, ensuring regular church attendance for both morning and evening services. The Ten Commandments were well understood and embraced by most, and a non-churched person likely understood the essence of the gospel message and accepted to some extent the authority of the Bible. In the public square, the primary religious discussion centered on what particular Christian denomination

---

[15] James 2:23

one would ultimately embrace. Would one chose the Methodist church or the Baptist church? Whatever choice was made, one would likely encounter a message of salvation by grace alone along with a common standard of moral behavior. All of this ensured that the pastor had a limited range of complexities to deal with, and these cultural boundaries gave the pastor a much more manageable world in which to serve. Accordingly, the congregation's expectations of the pastor were far more predictable and manageable.

This is not to say that pastors in times past did not have a difficult challenge ahead of them. People certainly held high expectations of their pastors. Weddings, funerals, and Sunday services rolled around with no less regularity. Nor did a cooperative culture release the pastor from the responsibility of teaching, preaching, caring, and counseling. One could quickly point out that this era forced upon pastors certain challenges that pastors today are no longer forced to confront. An African American pastor in the segregated south would describe these times as much less than idyllic. Women sensing a calling into ministry would certainly question the simplicity of these times. Yet for the average pastor, the expectations and demands of ministry life were generally considered reasonable and manageable.

How differently the modern pastor sees the landscape of pastoral ministry. Change, both culturally and religiously, has transformed the pastoral panorama into something far less recognizable and frighteningly less manageable. In the period of a few generations, new words have found their place of prominence in the lexicon of the culture. Communications technology, moral relativism, consumerism, mental illness, biblical illiteracy, fractured family systems, worship wars, globalization, theological relativism, political correctness, upward mobility, terrorism, urbanization, gender identity, syncretism, multiculturalism, fundamentalist extremism, and post-modern thought are just the starting point of an expanding dictionary of contemporary terms. These words shape the "new normal." But this "new normal" means an increased load of stress, pressure, and anxiety for the pastor and the local congregation.

What Changed? Major Cultural Shifts Affecting the Church Today

How did it come to be this way? What has happened in the span of a century or so to place the church within the midst of such uncertainty? In the sections to follow, I will examine the major historical and cultural developments affecting the contemporary pastor. Armed with this understanding, pastors and congregations can begin to rise above the influential forces of shifting culture shaping the church and pastoral ministry today.

The Enlightenment and the Modern World

The authors of the book, *Missional Church*, provide a helpful explanation of the tectonic shifts that have taken place in North American culture over the last five hundred years. The waves of societal change we see today began rippling deep below the surface during the Enlightenment of 16th and 17th century Europe. Fueled by the rise of humanism in the centuries before and by the Protestant Reformation itself, intellectuals of the Enlightenment fought against the restrictive authorities of both the monarchy and church hierarchy. Copernicus and Galileo, the well-known personalities at the inauguration of this shift, invoked rational thinking within the observable material world to advance a theory that the earth rotated around the sun. This observation stood contrary to the stated belief of the church and to the authority of the sacred scripture. This intellectual and political conflict between the Enlightenment and the church marked the first of many shots fired against the church's central authority. In the following centuries, Bacon, Descartes, Locke, and others contributed to the final demise of the old standard of authority—church tradition and divine revelation—and established the new authority for knowing—rational logic and human experience.[16]

With the authority of the church and its traditions now entirely suspect, and with the ultimate source of truth lying within the reason and logic of each human mind, there came a "renewed emphasis on the individual" and "personal freedom."[17] The autonomous individual, no longer directed by institutional authority, was now self-directed. As Stanley Genz says it, "The modern ideal champions the autonomous self, the self-determining subject who exists outside any tradition or community."[18] This embrace of the individual and his primacy over the central authority of institutions led to a radical shift in nearly every aspect of culture and invoked a major reshaping of the church.

In *Missional Church*, the authors identify the effects of the Enlightenment upon three key areas: truth, self, and society.[19] The view of truth changed, defined now by human reason and rationality rather than the edicts of institutional authorities.[20] Self changed as one's identity, once defined by one's relationship to the monarchy or the church, was now defined through rationality and autonomy. And society changed, moving from a hierarchical model controlled by rule of sovereigns to a

---

[16] Darrell L. Guder and Lois Barrett, *Missional Church* (Grand Rapids: William B. Eerdmans Pub. Co, 1998), 21-22.

[17] Guber, *Missional Church*, 20-21.

[18] Stanley Grenz, *A Primer on Postmodernism* (Grand Rapids: William B. Eerdmans Pub. Co, 1996), 4.

[19] Guder, *Missional Church*, 20-21.

[20] Guder, *Missional Church*, 21.

more democratic society that preserved the value of personal freedom and worked towards the common good.[21] While these developments faced strong opposition from the established church (the church's war on Galileo stands as a prime example), a new expression of Christianity, born from the Reformation, welcomed the deconstruction of the church's authority and adapted to modernity's freedom and individuality.[22] While modernity as a whole looked suspiciously at any world that could not be directly observed (i.e., the supernatural), the church came to use those same pillars of rational logic and human experience to develop rationally acceptable theologies[23] and new, decentralized church structures. Through the Reformation and a decentralized church, Christianity would weather the storm of modernity and in some respects embrace quite comfortably its core tenets.[24]

The Rise of Postmodernism

But what many in the modern period assumed was a new and stable method for knowing turned out to be the driving force behind a powerful pendulum that drove its way through the 20th century into today's contemporary culture. Beginning in the late 19th century with the writings of Friedrich Nietzsche and gaining full cultural steam by the 1970s, a new, reactionary impulse emerged to dismantle the ideals of modernity.[25] Termed "postmodernism,"[26] this philosophy was "unwilling

---

[21] Guder, *Missional Church*, 24

[22] Reggie McNeal, *The Present Future: Six Tough Questions for the Church* (San Francisco: Jossey-Bass, 2003), 54. McNeal refers to the Reformation here as "the spiritual counterpart to the Enlightenment."

[23] Henry Ruf, *Postmodern Rationality, Social Criticism, and Religion* (St. Paul, MN: Paragon House, 2005), 4-5. Ruf points out that religion in the hands of the modernist lead to much more of a "philosophical theology" that eliminated many of the mystical and social aspects of religion.

[24] McNeal, *The Present Future*, 54-55. McNeal argues that the North American church is "thoroughly modern." He points to a few examples: "[The church] has reduced its understanding of spirituality to numbers that can be reported (the triumph of materialism over spirit). A church is doing well if membership, giving, and facility square footage are increasing. The church is print reliant. The Bible has become for the modern church the supreme manifestation of the Word of God (not Christ) because it is 'objective truth' (a modern distinction).... The sermon (an explanation of the text) has replaced the mass (along with the mystery of God's intervention). Preaching reflects a Newtonian world, approaching the text as a body to be dissected into shreds of words and even parts of words (exegesis).... Sunday 'school' reflects the basic assumption that the path to Christian maturity involves the acquisition of biblical information."

[25] Grenz, *A Primer on Postmodernism*, 5.

[26] Tim Woods, *Beginning Postmodernism* (Manchester: Manchester University Press, 1999), 3, 6. The description of postmodernism that follows defines its effects in admittedly sharp terms; yet postmodernism is a somewhat ambiguous term when one

to allow the human intellect to serve as the sole determiner of what we should believe," and looked to "nonrational ways of knowing, conferring heightened status on the emotions and intuition."[27] What modernity helped to make so clear in terms of self, truth, and society, postmodernity rejected. The foundations of truth and reality were shaken. One scholar has described the difference between modernism and postmodernism this way:

> Modernists say that we must stay with the notion of rationality that many philosophers have accepted for hundreds and thousands of years. That tradition claims that all ideas of truth, knowledge, justice, goodness, beauty, good reasoning have remained and must remain the same throughout human history and must be applicable in every cultural and social setting. For the past 150 years, however, existentialists, pragmatists and so-called "postmodernist" thinkers have denied this claim and instead have claimed that all standards and norms, even those of rationality itself, are not sacred gods to be worshiped, but social products of human constitution at certain historical moments in the development of human forms of life.[28]

As a result, truth, self and society changed once again. Truth, which was believed to be attained through a rational and scientific inquiry safely guarded by trusted institutions, was now viewed as a relative, moving target shaped by manipulative, political, and institutional forces.[29] Since truth and certainty were thrown into doubt, the view of self was altered once again. The individual could no longer trust his or her ability to make rational and self-determined choices;[30] therefore, the idea that the individual was ever truly in control of his or her actions was diminished, driven now by subconscious, societal pressures beyond one's control.[31] With truth and self redefined, a new concept of society followed right in

---

seeks to reduce it to definition. As Woods puts it, "In all definitions, postmodernism has proved to be a snake-like concept whose twists and coils are difficult to pin down."

[27] Grenz, *A Primer on Postmodernism*, 14.

[28] Ruf, *Postmodern Rationality, Social Criticism, and Religion*, 7-8.

[29] Gentz, *A Primer on Postmodernism*, 6. Stanley Grenz describes the Michel Foucalt's assertion that not only is truth not attainable with any certainty, but any claim to have ascertained "'knowledge' is always the result of the use of power" and that "social institutions inevitably engage in violence when they impose their own understanding on the centerless flux of understanding."

[30] Sigmund Freud, Karl Marx, and others cast into doubt whether an individual can really make rationally determined choices at all. Freud argued that the individual was driven by unconscious forces within the mind. Marx argued that the forces of industry and economic class warfare determined the fate of the individual, not the other way around.

[31] Guber, *Missional Church*, 42.

line. With modernity's emphasis on the individual now seeming quite out of fashion in a postmodern world, the importance of community rose prominently in the collective conscience. Since the individual can make neither a serious claim to truth nor can rise above the societal forces around it, the individual could only hope to contribute to the truth knowledge of the larger community itself.[32]

This transformation of society and Western thought devastated a church that had built its theologies on a confidence in rationality and reason. The church, which had become quite comfortable breathing the air of the modern world, now found its legs knocked out from under it once again. Seen now as one of the "institutions" driven by power and rooted in inflexible claims of truth, the church came to be seen as a relic of modernity. The source of Christianity's objective truth, the Bible, was relegated to fable status. Furthermore, the church's embrace of foundational truth moved it from a respected center of society to its "narrow-minded" edges.[33]

As Christianity's authority diminished, a new religious diversity emerged. With the diversity of community as the only hope for finding truth or meaning, this merging of ideas led to a more pluralistic and syncretistic form of religious thought.[34] The postmodern world gave equal weight to all forms of religious, cultural, and philosophical expressions, since none alone could be trusted to produce ultimate truth. Postmoderns, then, became quite comfortable embracing often contradictory styles of thought (whether religious, spiritual, philosophical, etc.), weaving them together into a higher "truth."[35] In turn, postmodernity continually confronted society with "a seemingly discordant polyphony of decontextualized voices."[36]

Not only does postmodern thought present a philosophically challenging environment for the church, but a practical challenge emerges as well. Postmodern philosophy, grounded in the community over the individual, emerged in a world that finds community itself in fast decline. As postmodern thought emerged, so did communication technology, mobilization, and globalization. Each did its part to erode the structural

---

[32] Grenz, *A Primer on Postmodernism*, 14.

[33] George M. Marsden, *Understanding Fundamentalism and Evangelicalism* (Grand Rapids: William B. Eerdmans, 1991), 99.

[34] McNeal, *The Present Future*, 57-58.

[35] For example, The Pew Research Center found, for instance, that a quarter of mainline Protestants believe in re-incarnation, that 13 percent of evangelicals believe in astrology, and that a third of black Protestants believe in the "evil eye." Pew Forum on Religion and Public Life, "Many Americans Mix Multiple Faith," (Washington DC: Pew Research Center, December 2009): 7, accessed January 10, 2011, http://www.pewforum.org/files/2009/12/multiplefaiths.pdf.

[36] Grenz, *A Primer on Postmodernism*, 20.

fabric of the very community the postmodern world needed in its quest for meaning. [37] It could be said this way: Modernity had community, but did not value it. Postmodernity valued community, but could not have it. Thus, "with this erosion, persons find themselves very alone. In this context, individualism is not so much a choice people make as a condition forced upon them."[38]

This disintegration of community in the postmodern world has nearly eliminated the extended family, fractured nuclear families, and has brought "rising divorce rates, increases in the number of single-parent households, the prevalence of two-income families, busy lifestyles, and diverse definitions of what constitutes a family."[39] The church not only is on the outside of the philosophical mainstream, but it ministers in a world struggling for healthy community.

Postmodern thought changed everything. The new view of truth undermined the Bible. The new view of self birthed a new moral relativism. The new view of society instituted an embrace of religious pluralism. And a world teaming with new technologies fractured the very community upon which postmodern thought depends. Each shift put the church at increasing odds with world around it, while, at the same time, left behind a world most in need of the church's ministry. Ultimately, Christianity found itself then and finds itself still today in an "ever increasing struggle to regain what has been lost and to re-establish relevance once again."[40]

Christianity's Cultural Influence: From the Center to the Fray

What was the end result of these tectonic shifts? In most practical terms, the church lost its place of dominant influence in the culture. As one writer puts it, "There is a crisis in the life of the churches of North America. The crisis, most simply put, is that the social function the churches once fulfilled in American life is gone."[41]

The catalyst for the inevitable "disestablishment" of the church rose hand in hand with the separation of church and state. Over time, the disestablishment of state-controlled religion moved religion into the private world and left the structures of culture to be shaped by secular

---

[37] Guber, *Missional Church*, 43.

[38] Guber, *Missional Church*, 43.

[39] Guber, *Missional Church*, 43.

[40] Andrew R. Irvine, *Between Two Worlds: Understanding and Managing Clergy Stress,* (London: Wellington House, 1997), 63.

[41] George R. Hunsberger and Craig Van Gelder, eds. *The Church Between Gospel and Culture: The Emerging Mission in North America,* (Grand Rapids: W.B. Eerdmans Pub. Co, 1996), xiii.

ideals.[42] The process was gradual. As church and state separation began taking hold in the colonies, the leading worldview in Colonial America remained predominantly Christian, and more specifically, Protestant.[43] Despite the diverse denominational expressions of Protestant Christianity that emerged in the early colonies, Christian churches collectively "took for granted their special place in shaping the social order."[44] This accounts for the fact that in much of America's history, a form of "functional Christendom"[45] placed the church at the center of public life and enabled the church to influence "policy, morals, and institutions, while building a host of private institutions under their control."[46]

During the twentieth century, however, the secularization of the culture neutralized and perhaps even marginalized Protestant Christianity's influence over society.[47] Secularization "disassociated" religious belief from the "social mechanisms of world structuring" and removed the supernatural from "the processes of public life."[48] A religious force that once was at the center of all that shaped American culture and values was now left to compete with an increasingly secularized world.

The New Culture: More Secular and More Religious

The secularization of American culture produced an unexpected irony that plays into the stresses upon today's church and its leaders. As Hamberg and Pettersson have pointed out in their study of the growth of

---

[42] Guber, *Missional Church*, 51.

[43] Hunsberger and Van Gelder, *The Church Between Gospel and Culture*, xiii. While it is difficult to capture all the effects of culture upon the 20th and 21st century church, given its many expressions (Catholic, mainline Protestant, mainstream evangelical, Pentecostal, etc.), the focus here is on the impact upon the mainstream evangelical church and the mainline Protestant church within the North American context. Hunsberger and Van Gelder argue in the introduction to their book that it is within these traditions that the effects are "most pronounced."

[44] Guber, *Missional Church*, 50.

[45] Guber, *Missional Church*, 48-49. While the term "Christendom" is normally used to mark the marriage between the Christian church and the legal arm of the state (they refer to this as "Constintinianism"), Guber, et al., broaden the term "Christendom" to include the comfortable place the church long held in North America culture or, in their words, "the resulting impact of the Christian church on the empire's dominant culture."

[46] Guber, *Missional Church*, 50.

[47] Marsden, *Understanding Fundamentalism*, 99. Marsden writes, "Evangelical religion was regarded as though it had been peripheral and hence all the more dispensable to American culture."

[48] Hunsberger and Van Gelder, *The Church Between Gospel and Culture*, 79-112. See Christopher Kaiser's chapter, "From Biblical Secularity to Modern Secularism," for an excellent summary of the secularization of society.

the religious marketplace, [49] the separation of church and state helped create a society that was more secular *and* more religious at the same time. James Twitchell interprets their study by pointing out that church/state separation not only secularizes the foundational structures of culture, but also functions to increase religious diversity and the quantity of religious expression in the countries where it is tried. The lack of official religion and government entanglement, he argues, allows a greater diversity of religious thought to thrive and grow. The "religious supply" goes up, competitive innovation ensues, religious demand increases, and participation (i.e. church attendance) rises. (See Figure 1).

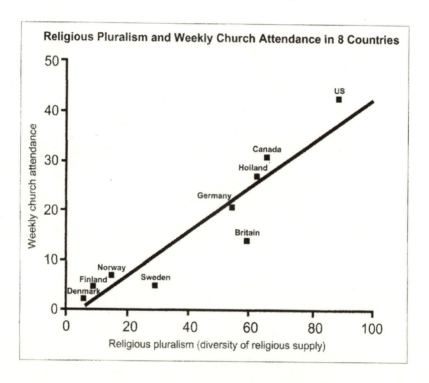

Figure 1: Hamberg and Pattersson's study reveals "an almost perfect relationship between religious pluralism and weekly church attendance."[50]

---

[49] Eva M. Hamberg and Thorlief Pettersson, "Religious Markets: Supply, Demand, Rational Choices," Ted G. Jelen, ed., *Sacred Markets, Sacred Canopies: Essays on Religious Markets and Religious Pluralism* (Oxford: Rowman & Littlefield Publishers, Inc., 2002), 91-114.
[50] Hamberg and Pattersson, *Religious Markets*, 108-109.

It is here that we begin to see the dynamics now affecting the contemporary church. First, the increasing secularism stole away the sense of power and influence the church once felt it had in shaping culture, instilling in Christians a sense of fear and antagonism about the culture at large. Second, the rise of so many competing religious expressions and ideas introduced yet another fear—that one's particular congregation could lose participants in the growing competition of religious ideas. It is these two factors—a secular society and a competitive religious environment—that shaped the church's response.

The Church's Response to a Changing World

In the beginning the church was a fellowship of men and women centering on the living Christ. Then the church moved to Greece, where it became a philosophy. Then it moved to Rome, where it became an institution. Next, it moved to Europe, where it became a culture. And, finally, it moved to America, where it became an enterprise.[51]

The move from the center of culture to its edges created the atmosphere of "enterprise" with which the church now struggles. A church still reeling from its loss of dominance in the culture suddenly found itself competing in an open marketplace of ideas. It is here that a new religious "competitive market spurs innovation and increases consumption."[52] This new environment placed a world of new pressures on the pastor. Local congregations, struggling to accept the new shape of religious life in America, could hardly escape the fear that culture was against it and that competing religious forces were sure to overtake it if action is not soon taken. The pastor was then called upon to lead the congregation against this rising tide and to produce results that would secure the local church against a frightening new world.

Because of the complexities of a society growing more secular and more religious at the same time, the church found itself growing more competitive on two fronts: with the culture and with other churches. In the sections to follow, I offer several issues contemporary in the church today that illustrate the competitive influences upon the church. With each of these issues, I hope to illuminate the recent and often abundant pressures that have been infused into the life of pastoral ministry.

---

[51] James B. Twitchell, *Shopping for God: How Christianity Went from in Your Heart to in Your Face*, (New York: Simon & Schuster, 2007), 20. Twitchell writes that this "famous quote [is] so on point that it has lost its specific source." It is traditionally attributed to Richard Halverson, former chaplain of the United States Senate.

[52] Twitchell, *Shopping for God*, 29.

Culture: The Competition Without

First is the church's growing competition against culture itself. I offer two general categories in which to think about the church's engagement with culture. One is confrontation. The other is accommodation.

Confronting the Culture: The Culture War

Many in the church have chosen to engage the culture with confrontation. The most obvious example is the culture war itself. A "Civil War of Values"[53] has landed squarely in the center of our churches today. The pressure is on to champion political platforms, endorse certain candidates, and confront certain cultural issues. The pastor is left to deal with a wide range of opinions—often within her own congregation—about the degree to which the church should be confrontational in its cultural temperament.

For some, this may stand as a fearful reaction to cultural change. For others, this approach has some deep and underlying theological motivations attached to it. Engaging in what is called Dominion Theology or Reconstructionism, some see the church as an agent of change called to transform earthly political structures in order to bring the world "under the authority of Jesus Christ."[54] Motivated by the vision of a Christianized civilization, Christians are called to be activists in the public realm in order to bring society in line with the law of God.[55] Given the increased secularization of society, many in the church have adopted this theological outlook, perhaps unknowingly, in hopes of winning back the church's influence in the culture once again.

The pastor is tasked with sifting through these expectations, certain to satisfy some while alienating others. Some pastors chose to step back from the culture war, questioning whether such an open confidence in the power of secular politics undermines personal confidence in the spiritual power of Christ and His Kingdom.[56] Others welcome the political battle

---

[53] James Dobson and Gary Bauer, *Children at Risk* (Dallas, TX: Word, Inc., 1990), 19-20.

[54] Paul N. Benware, *Understanding End Times Prophecy: A Comprehensive Approach* (Chicago: Moody Press, 1995), 150.

[55] Benware, *Understanding End Times Prophecy*, 150.

[56] Laurie Goodstein, "Disowning Conservative Politics, Evangelical Pastor Rattles Flock," *New York Times*, July 30, 2006, accessed December 2, 2010, http://www.nytimes.com/2006/07/30/ us/30pastor.html. Rev. Gregory A Boyd, a mega-church pastor of Woodland Hills Church, publically stated in 2006 that he would not endorse a political candidate and that the church would "steer clear of politics," saying "When [the church] conquers the world, it becomes the world." The *New York Times* reported that "by the time the dust settled, Woodland Hills, which Mr. Boyd founded in 1992, had lost about 1,000 of its 5,000 members."

and fight it proudly as a means of instituting biblical change in the world.[57] Whichever position the pastor chooses to take, he is certain to face an emotionally charged conflict within the congregation as the issue of cultural engagement plays itself out.

Accommodating the Culture: The Church Growth Movement

Another popular approach—one with even more complexities and challenges for the pastor—seeks to accommodate to the ways of culture in order to win it back. Many have chosen to embrace the culture as far as is ethically possible in the programming and design of its ministries in order to connect with the culture in a positive way. This has certainly been the primary strategy of the "church growth movement" that began to sweep through the halls of Protestant Christianity some fifty years ago. This movement "focused on reaching persons outside the church to incorporate them into the church."[58] It seeks to make the church as attractive as possible, luring in those who have found the church irrelevant or locked in lifeless traditionalism.

Reggie McNeal, in his book *The Present Future*, describes and evaluates the church growth movement and its effect on American Christianity in general and pastors in particular. Founded on the belief that church growth was a natural result of a church's commitment to Great Commission principles, pastors were trained to position new churches in various growth areas around major cities, to practice homogeneous principles of attraction, to employ business principles of marketing and organization, and to exegete and understand the culture.[59] Ministry success came to be defined by increased numbers, attractive programs, new buildings, and growing staff rather than the intangible measurements of the spiritual world.[60]

As this new approach offered a renewed hope in the church's battle with the culture, a troubling pressure began to build on pastors and church leaders.[61] McNeal describes it this way:

> …[C]hurch leaders didn't know how to deal with a church that moved away from a privileged position to a church in exile in an increasingly alien culture. Tending to church members who were bewildered at the cultural shifts was draining enough, but to add

---

[57] Marsden, *Understanding Fundamentalism*, 107. Marsden underscores one such viewpoint: "[M]any fundamentalists tended to view politics primarily as signs of the times pointed toward the early return of Jesus to set up a political kingdom in the land of Israel."

[58] Guder, *Missional Church*, 73.

[59] McNeal, *The Present Future*, 21-22.

[60] McNeal, *The Present Future*, 54.

[61] Rediger, *Clergy Killers*, 23.

pressure to grow to the list of expectations of church leadership proved too much for many. They felt as though they were doing well just to hang on to what they had…."[62]

He further adds,

> Central to church growth teaching was an admonition that church leaders should assume responsibility for the growth of the church, and, as a corollary, if a church isn't growing it is being disobedient to God, falling short of his expectations.[63]

The church growth movement inadvertently placed a new set of pressures on pastors. Congregations came to see their pastor as a CEO styled leader, expected to understand and successfully translate business and marketing strategies into the world of the church.[64] The pastor became the primary marketer of "religious goods and services,"[65] living with an accompanying pressure to master the latest in technology, programming, study resources, and methodology. One observer states that if attendance did not increase as a result, "little attention is paid to the cultural and societal dynamics affecting the current attendance level and the responsibility is laid at the feet of the clergy," further adding that the pressure on clergy for increased church attendance "encapsulates the unrealistic expectations of a desperate church afraid to face the issues of relevance in a changing world."[66]

Many have offered and will continue to offer evaluations of both the culture war and the church growth movement. The mention of these here is not to be considered an evaluation of these trends, for as with most developments in church history, time will continue to reveal both their contributions and their shortcomings. What remains relevant here is the role that cultural engagement has played in the increasing pressures, stresses, and expectations now hoisted onto the life and work of the pastor.

Christianity: The Competition Within

It is more than merely the secularization of the culture that began to shape contemporary ecclesiology. Increasingly, a growing competition began rising within Christianity itself as the number of religious options began to outpace the number of available participants. This too requires a brief look at several pressing issues.

---

[62] McNeal, *The Present Future*, 21-22.
[63] McNeal, *The Present Future*, 21.
[64] McNeal, *The Present Future*, 24. See also Rediger, *Clergy Killers*, 20.
[65] Guber, *Missional Church*, 84.
[66] Irvine, *Between Two Worlds*, 75.

Church Growth and Inter-Congregational Competition

One pressing issue involves once again the church growth movement. The church growth movement not only represented the church's response to the culture, but it unintentionally helped to foster the competition growing among churches themselves.[67] Because the church growth movement appeared successfully to direct the church away from a state of decline towards a state of renewal, nearly every aspect of church life—from music to Sunday School to programming to dress to architecture—came under scrutiny and modernization. Each church had to address the question, would the church continue in the traditions of earlier days or embrace more fashionable and contemporary ideas?

The side effects of this debate are numerous. Initially, the culture-friendly, "seeker-sensitive" methods of the church growth movement (contemporary music, entertaining programming, cutting edge communications technology, specialized staff, etc.) were aimed at stimulating the interests of people uninterested in church. Yet Christians too came to embrace and expect these engaging religious options for themselves, not just for the unchurched. Christians became "high-maintenance church consumer[s],"[68] and churches that did not employ these new seeker-friendly methods fell behind as consumer minded church members shopped their membership out to churches offering more fashionable programming.[69]

Adding to this complexity was the rise of the megachurch. The megachurch phenomenon arose in response to the population's shift away from small "mom-and-pop operations" to the "supercenter."[70] Soon, many churches found themselves living in the shadows of these super-sized congregations. Clearly, pastors have benefited from the insights gleaned from the success of the megachurch, but many have also suffered a loss of members to them as well. "With rare exception the 'growth' here was the cannibalization of the smaller membership churches by these emerging supercenters" in what McNeal calls "the migration of Christians moving from one church to another."[71] Some congregations grew exponentially, while other congregations lacking the right location and attractive culture-friendly techniques were left to suffer membership losses. McNeal once again captures the trouble for many pastors:

> The rise of the celebrity-status church culture… has created
> thousands of "losers," pastors and church leaders who are not

---

[67] McNeal, *The Present Future*, 24.
[68] McNeal, *The Present Future*, 24.
[69] London and Wiseman, *Pastors at Greater Risk*, 43.
[70] McNeal, *The Present Future*, 22.
[71] McNeal, *The Present Future*, 22.

serving in high-profile, high-growth churches. Consequently, a larger part of the leadership of the North American church suffers from debilitation and even depression fostered by a lack of significance. The army of God has a lot of demoralized leaders.[72]

Ultimately, committed pastors are caught between competing expectations, seeking both to satisfy the older faithful while reaching the next generation.

> This creates for the clergy incredible stressors. There is the need to accommodate the older faithful church attenders, often the majority of a greying church population, who have financially supported the institution and are happy with the church as conveyer of yesterday's standards and values. On the other hand, there is the need to make the teaching relevant to the changing world view of today's generation. The clergy become caught in the intergenerational cross-fire.[73]

Theological Conflict

A second inescapable issue promoting conflict among churches and bringing a new measure of stress for pastors is the continuous theological conflict of the last century or more. Documenting the hostilities within the church, renowned historian, George Marsden, traces the conflict back to Charles Darwin's *Origen of Species* and the rise of German higher criticism. Both challenged the integrity and reliability of the Bible. The Bible–something of "crucial importance" to the "nineteenth century American evangelical's whole way of thinking"–was demythologized into an undependable source of truth. The church divided over its response.[74]

The conflict produced two broad streams within the church. One sought to accommodate the teachings of the Bible to this new information (theological liberalism), while the other stood against any and all forms of accommodation (theological fundamentalism or conservativism). These two competing views of the Bible's authority have continued to run parallel throughout the 20th into the 21st century, albeit with varying adaptations and alterations. As a result, each new theological issue emerged with even greater force and division. Whether it was evolution / creation debate, the inerrancy issue, the social justice movement, the battle over millennial viewpoints, the acceptance of new versions of the Bible, or the emergence of dispensational theology, each issue drew new lines of demarcation between and within churches,

---

[72] McNeal, *The Present Future*, 23.
[73] Irvine, *Between Two Worlds*, 71-72.
[74] Marsden, *Understanding Fundamentalism*, 12-13.

movements, and denominations. Today, the ordination of women and the issue of homosexuality are two of such issues which continue to stoke the ecclesiastical conflict to the point where many denominations continue to splinter. [75]

The pastor leads in a time of continuous theological conflict. While much of this conflict may be entirely necessary, the emotionally charged nature of each issue has the potential to put pastors at odds not only with people in their own congregation, but also with fellow pastors and denominational leaders with whom a pastor would normally find support. Few pastors can escape the tensions and pressures that many theological issues bring.

As I bring to a close the description of the many forces descending upon the church today, it must be said that the practical challenges of the pastorate are even more than what could be offered here. Ministry involves heavy involvement with people, time demands from family and work, the pedestal of high expectations, financial pressures, pastors' high tendency towards perfectionism, the constant entanglement of professional and personal life, and what one study showed to be an overall "diminished quality of life" for pastors and their families compared to lay people in the church.[76] In another study, pastors listed time, boundaries, isolation, conflict, mobility, life in the parsonage, concern for children and spouse, and family dynamics as top sources of stress.[77] More still, London and Wiseman managed to list twenty hazards of ministry ranging from the hectic pace of modern life to suffocating level of expectations.[78] These surveys and studies call the committed pastor to a state of awareness regarding the negative effects these many sources of stress can have on his or her own personal health.

The Health of the Contemporary Pastor

Clergy health suffers when these high pressure conflicts continue unabated. Much of the outworking of this pressure emerges in the form of stress and burnout, which are increasingly on the rise among pastors.[79]

---

[75] Marsden, *Understanding Fundamentalism*, 101. As Marsden states, "The chief question dividing the [evangelical] movement was whether true Christians ought to separate from unbelief and form their own churches." Many churches decided that "[t]hey should separate into pure churches and preach the gospel for the higher cause that eternal souls would be saved for eternity."

[76] Janelle Warner and John D. Carter, "Loneliness, Marital Adjustment and Burnout in Pastoral and Lay Persons," *Journal of Psychology and Theology* 12, no. 2 (1984): 131.

[77] Clergy Center of Pastors Institute and Department of Family and Child Services at Florida State University, *The Bridge* (February 28, 2001), quoted in London and Wiseman, *Pastors at Greater Risk*, 172.

[78] London and Wiseman, *Pastors at Greater Risk*, 37-58.

[79] London and Wiseman, *Pastors at Greater Risk*, 173.

Burnout is a "progressive loss of idealism, energy, and purpose experienced by people in the helping professions."[80] Or simply, "Burnout is a word we use when a person has become exhausted with his or her profession or major life activity."[81] Roy Oswald of the Alban Institute provides a helpful distinction between stress and burnout, noting, "Stress taxes our adjustment capacities, while burnout taxes our ability to continue caring."[82] Sustained levels of stress over a long period of time inevitably move the pastor from a state of stress to a place of burnout.[83] By understanding how stress and burnout occur, one can begin to see how these broad cultural and philosophical movements threaten the pastor's health.

Hatcher and Underwood, in their study of Southern Baptist pastors, suggest that burnout begins in the pastor's low self-esteem. Their study revealed that ministers with lower self-concepts have higher levels of anxiety and a greater inability to cope with that anxiety. Given that 70 percent of pastors report having a lower self-image after being in pastoral ministry than when they started, the potential for pastors to buckle under stress is high.[84]

Miner, Sterland, and Dowson help to identify the major causes of this reduced self-image. Rising secularism and the increasing church competition documented earlier are major factors in this diminished self-concept. In their recent study, they demonstrate that secularism—being the decreased influence of religion on society—produces in pastors "the loss of social legitimation of ministry work."[85] Outside sources in the culture once provided the pastor with respect, social standing, and "legitimation."[86] Given the church's loss of status in the culture, it

---

[80] Jerry Edelwich and Archie Brodsky, *Burnout – Stages of Disillusionment in the Helping Professions* (New York: Human Sciences Press, 1980); quoted in Oswald, *Clergy Self-Care*, 59.

[81] John A. Sanford, *Ministry Burnout* (Louisville, KY: Westminster/John Knox Press, 1982), 1.

[82] Roy M Oswald, *Clergy Self-Care: Finding a Balance For Effective Ministry* (Washington, DC: Alban Institute, 1991), 58.

[83] Christine Maslach, *Burnout: The Cost of Caring* (Englewood Cliffs, NJ: Prentice-Hall, Inc., 1982), 11. Maslach states that "the burnout syndrome appears to be a response to chronic everyday stress (rather than to occasional crisis)."

[84] "1991 Survey of Pastors," Fuller Church Growth Institute, quoted in London and Wiseman, *Pastors at Greater Risk*, 172.

[85] Maureen Miner, Sam Sterland, and Martin Dowson. "Orientation to the Demands of Ministry: Construct Validity and Relationship with Burnout," *Review of Religious Research* 50, no. 4 (2009): 465.

[86] John Scott and Gordon Marshall, *Oxford Dictionary of Sociology* (Oxford: Oxford University Press, 2005), 358-359. Legitimation is a sociological term that refers to "the process by which power is not only institutionalized but more importantly is given moral grounding." The loss of the pastor's legitimation is not in the loss of institutional power, per se, but the loss of "moral grounding" or authoritative standing in the culture.

naturally follows that a loss of stature for the pastor would occur as well.[87] The fact that the pastor is no longer a respected authority in society produces a negative psychological effect.[88] As one pastor and scholar puts it, "Clergy, who were at one time viewed by most as equal in authority to the doctor and educator, and by some as superior to these for—after all, they represented the Divine—have been virtually stripped of all influence."[89]

Given the lack of cultural legitimation, pastors naturally turn to their congregations for support. This too brings about its own set of issues. As Miner, Sterland, and Dowson put it,

> …[T]his source of legitimation is unstable as it varies with the performance of the minister and the composition and disposition of the congregation. Hence, ministers seeking external legitimation from their congregations may experience declines in self-esteem, autonomy, control, and role clarity associated with inconsistent or negative external feedback…."[90]

Echoing the difficulty pastors have in finding legitimation from their congregations, Roy Oswald points out that for many pastors,

> …[T]he message they hear from the church at all levels—and from themselves—is "you can do more" and "you can do it better." Few voices ask, "Are you having any fun lately?" "What is happening to your relationships as a result of your ministry?" "What impact has your ministry had on your body?" "Where are you getting spiritual feeding?"[91]

Adding to the loss of legitimation from the culture and from the congregation itself, pastors can often be their own worst critics.[92] Pastors are more likely to place unrealistic demands on themselves, strive towards perfectionism, and maintain higher levels of self-criticism,[93] leading to an additional set of stress-inducing behaviors, including taking on unrealistic workloads, failing to define boundaries, not taking time off, and accepting unrealistic standards of success.[94]

---

[87] Irvine, *Between Two Worlds*, 62.

[88] Miner, "Orientation to the Demands of Ministry," 465.

[89] Irvine, *Between Two Worlds*, 54.

[90] Miner, "Orientation to the Demands of Ministry," 465.

[91] Oswald, *Clergy Self-Care*, ix.

[92] Irvine, *Between Two Worlds*, 35.

[93] S. Wayne Hatcher and Joe Ray Underwood, "Self-Concept and Stress: A Study of a Group of Southern Baptist Ministers," *Counseling and Values* 34, no. 3 (April 1990): 193.

[94] Irvine, *Between Two Worlds*, 27-36.

Together, these behaviors push the pastor into a self-defeating cycle. As a pastor's self-esteem drops, he becomes less equipped to deal with ongoing stress. The pastor finds himself "at the mercy of the surrounding situation instead of shaping and controlling it," resulting in a "greater chance of being overburdened and emotionally depleted."[95] As stress grows, Oswald points out, one experiences a decrease in perception, an inability to see available options, a regression towards infantile behavior, a progression towards destructive relationship patterns, as well as increases in fatigue, depression, and physical illness.[96] These "self-destructive patterns"[97] are fuel for the cycle. High stress results in decreased abilities which lowers ones self-image which then produces even higher levels of stress which leads to a further decline in self-concept.[98] The effects of this cycle are compounded as caring professionals can easily "pour in much more than they get back from their clients, supervisors, and colleagues."[99] Pastoring is a lifestyle of continuous giving. Without replenishing the self, the stress cycle advances on. In the end, failure to deal with high levels of stress pushes pastors across what Oswald calls the "stress threshold"–the point at which the stress becomes destructive.[100] As pastors cross this threshold, pastors begin to "blow out."[101] Christine Maslash describes the effects of burnout in relationship to the caring profession in general, a description which resounds clearly through the life of the clergy.

> The emotional exhaustion and cynicism of burnout are often accompanied by a deterioration in physical and psychological well-being. Relationships with other people suffer, both on and off the job.... The burned-out provider is prone to health problems, psychological impairment, loss of self-esteem, and a growing dissatisfaction with the job.[102]

While stress and burnout are psychological descriptions of what occurs when pressures on the pastor go unrelieved, these stresses can also work themselves out in ways destructive to the moral and professional reputation of today's clergy. Whether it is the nearly quarter of all clergy

---

[95] Maslach, *Burnout: The Cost of Caring*, 63.

[96] Oswald, *Clergy Self-Care*, 44-47.

[97] Oswald, *Clergy Self-Care*, ix.

[98] Hatcher and Underwood, "Self-Concept and Stress," 193.

[99] Ayala M. Pines, Elliot Aronson, and Ditsa Kafry, *Burnout: From Tedium to Personal Growth* (New York: The Free Press, 1981), 3.

[100] Oswald, *Clergy Self-Care*, 39-43.

[101] Oswald, *Clergy Self-Care*, 44. Oswald offers several stress self-assessment tools for determining this threshold.

[102] Maslach, *Burnout: The Cost of Caring*, 73.

who have been forced to resign at some point in their ministry,[103] the third of pastors who admit to inappropriate sexual behavior with someone in the church,[104] the 20 percent who admit to having had an extramarital affair, the half who admit that internet pornography is a real temptation,[105] or the nearly quarter of pastors who have required marital counseling,[106] the portrait of the contemporary pastor is a troubled one. A pastor without an intentional strategy for coping with the demands of ministry will find himself subsumed—often unwittingly—within these frightening numbers.

How Does a Pastor Survive?

We return full circle to the question with which we began. With the seismic shift from modern to postmodern culture, the growing competition within church life, the growing expectations of the pastor, and the resulting increase in burnout, the question now carries even greater significance: how does a pastor drape himself with the proper safeguards so as to persevere in the midst of such inevitable struggles? The pastoral support system is significant to this task. A pastoral support system[107] is a series of intentional practices and supportive relationships that serve as "dependable sources of healing, defense, guidance, and prevention of abuse."[108] Both individual and interpersonal in nature, this "anchor in a windstorm"[109] helps to preserve, retool, and care for the needs of the pastoral caregiver.

---

[103] London and Wiseman, *Pastors at Greater Risk*, 34.

[104] London and Wiseman, *Pastors at Greater Risk*, 20.

[105] This and the previous statistic from London and Wiseman, *Pastors at Greater Risk*, 238.

[106] This and the previous statistic from London and Wiseman, *Pastors at Greater Risk*, 86.

[107] The specific term, "pastoral support system," can be found under other names with as many variations in structure and purpose. Irvine (*Between Two Worlds*, 160ff) takes a more professional view, describing many different "models of support" available to the pastor. Specifically, he looks to neighboring professions (doctors, lawyers, teachers, etc.) and their professional organizations which provide "training, set standards, determine professional ethics, provide criteria for entrance to the profession and deal with concerns of the group in general" as the model for a pastoral support group. Oswald (*Clergy Self-Care*, 129ff) is more informal in his concept of support structure, emphasizing that "the most helpful support systems are those that allow [the clergy] to be 'out of role' for a time." Few define exactly what constructs a support system, leaving the clergy member to customize the support system that most meets his or her needs. London and Wiseman (*Pastors at Greater Risk*) make no mention of a support system, choosing to focus on individual steps a pastor can take to sidestepping pitfalls and avoiding burnout.

[108] Rediger, *Clergy Killers*, 147.

[109] Oswald, *Clergy Self-Care*, 129.

Internal Legitimation and Personal Support Relationships

Miner, Sterland, and Dowson lay the groundwork for the importance of support systems. In acknowledging that external sources of legitimation are now in limited supply, the researchers suggest that a pastor must "modify ministry orientation" from external sources (society and congregation) to internal sources. Pastors cannot expect for legitimation to be delivered to them from outside sources, but they instead must seek out that legitimation in other ways. They define these internal sources as spiritual connectedness, competence, and autonomy.[110]

Spiritual connectedness grounds the minister's calling in the work of God and His ongoing sovereign direction. The ongoing commitment to spiritual connectedness can mitigate against personal faith struggles that are more prevalent in a pluralistic society. It further affirms a pastor's larger sense of calling in the midst of low points of ministry, bringing affirmation of one's work from God and not from temperamental sources.[111] Retreats, spiritual disciplines, regular Bible study, meditation, journaling, and engaging a spiritual director are a few such strategies to strengthen one's spiritual connectedness to God.[112] The researchers demonstrate that ministers who have a suitable level of spiritual connectedness develop a greater sense of authority for their ministry and a healthier, more enduring, inner strength.[113]

Competence is another internal source of legitimation that promotes a confidence independent of external affirmation. As one grows in her skills as a minister, the pastor will more likely feel confident in making difficult leadership decisions, despite the abundance of external and often contradictory demands coming at the pastor.[114] Achieved through a commitment to self-help, counseling, peer mentoring relationships, continuing and advanced education, etc., a pastor can increase his credibility and ability to meet the many challenges present in today's complex environment.[115]

Finally, a sense of autonomy is the development of a clear sense of self that will enable a pastor to transcend any "dependence on congregational support and encouragement."[116] Not to be confused with self-sufficiency, it is the "capacity to act with and for others out of a well-developed sense of self."[117] A strong sense of autonomy provides the kind

---

[110] Miner, Sterland, and Dowson, "Orientation to the Demands of Ministry," 466.
[111] Miner, Sterland, and Dowson, "Orientation to the Demands of Ministry," 465.
[112] Oswald, *Clergy Self-Care*, 96ff.
[113] Miner, Sterland and Dowson, "Coping with Ministry," 227.
[114] Miner, Sterland and Dowson, "Coping with Ministry,"227.
[115] Miner, Sterland, and Dowson, "Orientation to the Demands of Ministry," 468.
[116] Miner, Sterland and Dowson, "Coping with Ministry," 217.
[117] Miner, Sterland and Dowson, "Coping with Ministry," 217.

of emotional stability that produces feelings of security about one's work and calling despite the external challenges pressing in on the pastor.

The development of these three internal sources of legitimation can help the pastor rise above the many movements and challenges and expectations present in ministry today. As Miner, Sterland and Dowson summarize it:

> A key point here is that if foundations of internal legitimation derived from spiritual relatedness, competence, and autonomy are lacking, a minister can only rely on potentially shifting and dwindling sources of external legitimation…. Those with a weak internal orientation to ministry…will exhibit increased levels of burnout as well as anxiety and depression indicative of existential insecurity. This insecurity may arise as ministers with weak internal orientations depend on insufficient, precarious internal supports, or fickle external supports, rather than on more stable inner spiritual or personal convictions to guide their responses to existential concerns. Conversely, those who respond to the pressures of secularization with a strong internal orientation to ministry will have a decreased risk of burnout and distress.[118]

Given the importance of a strong internal orientation in pastors, Miner, Sterland, and Dowson encourage also the use of supportive relationships in developing ones personal sense of legitimacy.[119] Collegial relationships, denominational associations, personal counselors, staff relationships, spiritual directors, accountability partners, and mentor relationships—woven together in an intentional network of support—can provide the pastor with the legitimacy, encouragement, and support that are often difficult to find through one's congregation or society or through "rugged individualism."[120] Spiritual connectedness with God is only improved as a spiritual director or accountability partner is brought into the process. The development of competencies depends on peer, collegial, mentor, educational, and denominational relationships. A sense of wholeness and autonomy is fortified when mentors or collegial relationships are introduced. Together this web of supportive relationships solidifies, affirms, and undergirds the pastor's personal sense of legitimacy amidst the arduous task of ministry.

In general, a system of supportive relationships can provide the pastor with the right perspective in the face of continual criticism or

---

[118] Miner, Sterland, and Dowson, "Orientation to the Demands of Ministry," 466.
[119] Miner, Sterland, and Dowson, "Orientation to the Demands of Ministry,"475-476.
[120] Rediger, *Clergy Killers*, 148.

leadership challenges. As Charles Chandler of the Ministering to Ministers Foundation says,

> A formal minister's support group can be a valuable asset to a minister at any time whether or not there are any crises. Tunnel vision becomes the norm when under severe pressure; so do feelings of isolation and inadequacy, denial, lack of trust, withdrawal, and a desire to run. A minister's support group can address many of these issues with a participant in a safe setting.[121]

Friendships in the Pastoral Support System

The question, however, remains open. Are a pastor's friendships worthy to be named as a necessary part of the pastor's network of supportive relationships? Is there a significant enough function within friendships to call pastors to develop and maintain friendships as a necessary strategy for enduring the hardships of ministry?

Bruce Reed, in his book, *The Dynamics of Religion*[122] provides a framework within which we begin to see the importance of the pastor's friendships in providing strength and legitimation for the pastor. Reed's model—something that will be explored in more detail in chapter five—speaks to the nature of oscillation. All persons oscillate between two worlds—the worlds of intra-dependence and extra-dependence. In the world of intra-dependence, one has a societal role to play, whether in one's job or family or community. In this world, one is intertwined in a network of dependent relationships where energy is spent contributing to the functioning of the greater system. In the state of extra-dependence, one escapes that role of "doing" into a state of "being." No longer intertwined into the world of intra-dependence, one can then retreat from his or her societal role, turn control over to someone else, be taken care of, reflect upon life, and simply "be." It is this state of extra-dependence that one is retooled and energized for reentry into the intra-dependent world.[123] Given the heavy intra-dependent role most pastors play in their congregations as well as the often extraordinary amount of time the pastor spends within that role, pastors experience too little time away from their care-giving roles. The pastoral support system provides the extra-

---

[121] Charles H. Chandler, "Five Relationships Every Minister Needs to Develop," (Richmond, VA: Ministering to Ministers Foundation, Inc., 2010): 1, accessed January 11, 2011, http://mtmfoundation.org/files/Five%20Relationships%20Every%20Minister%20Needs%20to%20Develop.pdf.

[122] Bruce D. Reed, *The Dynamics of Religion: Process and Movement in Christian Churches* (London: Darton, Longman and Todd, 1978).

[123] Oswald, *Clergy Self-Care*, 130-135. Oswald helps translate Reed's model into the pastor's personal support system.

dependence a pastor needs away from the messy and complex world of ministry.

It is in Reed's model that the significance of friendships emerges. Friendships allow more than any other relationship for the pastor to be completely "out of role."[124] Friendships may appear on the surface to be an optional luxury given the sometimes nebulous and diluted state of friendships today, but for pastors, friendships afford them with a much needed escape from their intense intra-dependent role. Collegial, denominational, and professional relationships indeed provide significant and necessary supports for the pastor, but within friendships, the pastor finds one of the few remaining places where he is entirely free to "be" instead of "do." [125] Other supportive relationships are generally connected to a pastor's role and place of ministry. Emphasizing the value of friendships in a time of ministry transition, Oswald points out that denominational and collegial relationships are most likely to fade when a pastor leaves his parish, but friendships often remain intact.[126]

Therefore, if friendships provide a meaningful and renewing escape from the pastoral role in a way few other relationships can, is it not important then for the pastor to include friendships as an intentional part of his support system? I contend that this oft-overlooked relationship can be a source of great support for the pastor and needs fresh attention in clergy circles. With this in view, I will seek to explore in the remaining chapters this challenging and often elusive relationship. How can these relationships that have been with us all our lives—often with little thought to how they were formed or what benefit they provided—be reframed into an intentional means of support? How can a renewed understanding of friendships provide the much-needed relief a pastor needs from the mounting demands of ministry?

Elijah: A Contemporary Crisis in Ancient Times

Before turning specifically to the nature of friendships and its place in the pastor's relational support system, it is worth reflecting on the insights of a biblical narrative that encapsulates the challenges that contemporary pastors face today and undergirds with biblical authority the need for a personal support system. Elijah, the prophet of Israel, was one such servant of God who persisted through a particularly demanding season of ministry. In a short period of time, Elijah proclaimed God's

---

124 Oswald, *Clergy Self-Care*, 134-135. Oswald urges the pastor to have "one or two friends" who will enable the pastor to "move completely into a state of Extra-dependence."

125 Certainly, friendships within the church make the escape from the clergy role much more complex and challenging, something addressed in more detail in chapter three.

126 Oswald, *Clergy Self-Care*, 136-137.

message to His people, challenged the prevailing cultural ideas, engaged outsiders like the widow at Zarephath, and confronted the powers of his day. While Elijah's calling took him to places most contemporary pastors have not gone (killing hundreds of false prophets and alluding death come to mind), pastors can indeed find themselves captured by Elijah's experience. For along with the host of ministry successes, Elijah came to struggle with the darker side of ministry. Like many a contemporary pastor, he faced a loss of social legitimacy, descended into suffocating burnout, withdrew into a season of recovery, engaged in a redefinition of success, and structured a new system of supportive relationships.

Elijah's story begins with a fast rise to the top. Beginning with a successful prediction of impending drought, followed by God's miraculous supply of food from a raven, and the multiplication of flour and oil for the widow at Zarephath, Elijah's confidence only increased when God delivered him from the king's murderous annihilation of the prophets of Israel. Armed with a vigorous confidence, Elijah pressed forward with his confrontation of the prophets of Baal and their destructive influences on God's people. As I Kings 18 details, Elijah concluded his confrontation with the king by challenging the prophets of Baal to a contest of spiritual power. This one remaining prophet of Yahweh arranged a contest against 450 prophets of Baal to see whose deity could rein down a fire from heaven to ignite a prepared sacrifice. With two altars arranged for the contest, the prophets of Baal initiated their religious ritual. After several rounds of dancing and ritual and bodily cutting in hopes of inciting their god to action, nothing happened. Out of Elijah's brimming confidence comes his response: "'Shout louder!' he said. 'Surely he is a god! Perhaps he is deep in thought, or busy, or traveling. Maybe he is sleeping and must be awakened.'"[127]

With no trace of weakness, Elijah called upon God's power to ignite a sacrifice soaked and saturated three times over until every each piece of wood was wet and the sacrificial bull was drenched. Placing his credibility and God's entirely on the line, Elijah invoked his prayer. The prophets of Baal looked on as "a fire of the LORD fell and burned up the sacrifice, the wood, the stones and the soil, and also licked up the water in the trench."[128] The victory not only led to the destruction of the prophets of Baal and a dramatic end to the severe drought, but to a mass public confession of the Lord as God.

With such a dramatic example of "ministry success" like few in ministry have ever known, what follows takes the reader completely by surprise. A few verses later, the reader is confronted with Elijah's

---

[127] I Kings 18:27
[128] I Kings 18:38

unexpected response: "[Elijah] came to a broom bush, sat down under it and prayed that he might die. 'I have had enough, LORD,' he said. 'Take my life; I am no better than my ancestors.'"[129] In a relatively short time, Elijah moves from a place of victory to the edge of burnout. What brought him to this dramatic and unexpected place so quickly?

Several clues in the narrative help us connect Elijah's sudden fall to the burnout conditions that many pastors face. Elijah experiences his own loss of legitimation. Though not explicit in the text, one could wonder if Elijah has assumed that a powerful mountaintop victory should restructure the king's way of thinking about God. As a result, Elijah perhaps imagines his own reputation growing in the king's eyes. Instead, King Ahab yields to his wife's disturbing conviction that the prophet must die for what he has done. Rather than have the legitimacy of his work affirmed, Elijah is now a hunted man.

Given Elijah's sudden loss of spiritual and emotional vigor, it is quite evident that he has placed great personal value in the responses of the political powers around him. Making the mistake that many a contemporary pastor has made, Elijah takes personal responsibility for the way others respond to God's work through him, failing to realize that those results rest only in the work of God himself. Elijah's unrealistic expectations of himself, the stress of Jezebel's threat, and the lack of affirmation from sources outside of God himself lead to Elijah's emotional collapse. Elijah's loss of legitimacy leads him into isolation and finally to physical collapse.

Elijah's exhaustion induces a rest that will mark the beginning of his restoration. Now fully exhausted, Elijah receives a visit from the Lord's messenger who initiates the renew process. Restoration begins with repeated pattern of eating and resting. Once physical strength is regained, his spirit begins its renewal. Invited into an encounter with God, Elijah learns that God's greatest work in his life comes not through the mighty and dramatic (symbolized by the presence of a great wind, earthquake, and fire), but in the "gentle whisper" of God's presence.[130]

Through his encounter with God, Elijah's role in God's work is redefined. Elijah discovers that he cannot bear the responsibility for what only God is responsible for. He learns that he cannot depend upon external powers of culture and kingship for the affirmation of his ministry. He realizes that the mountaintop moments are not what feed him, but that God's "gentle whisper" is what nurtures him. He comes to accept that he cannot sustain an intense period of ministry without physical rest and renewal.

---

[129] I Kings 19:4b-5
[130] I Kings 19:12

Most importantly, Elijah recognizes that his own health depends not on controlling his circumstances, but about finding personal strength in the midst of those circumstances. Interestingly, Elijah is given an opportunity to describe his circumstances, both before and after his encounter with God. Elijah gives an identical response: "I have been very zealous for the LORD God Almighty. The Israelites have rejected your covenant, torn down your altars, and put your prophets to death with the sword. I am the only one left, and now they are trying to kill me too."[131] Given that God's gentle whisper washes over Elijah in between his double recitation of his circumstances, one might hope for something new to emerge from Elijah's lips–perhaps a more positive spin on what he is about to face. Instead, the narrator emphasizes that despite Elijah's powerful and renewing encounter with God, Elijah must return to circumstances that are no better than they were when he left them. God specifically tells Elijah to "go back the way you came,"[132] emphasizing that he must tread the same path that brought him to the point of exhaustion. The difference is in what has changed: not Elijah's circumstances, but Elijah himself.

God does change one particular circumstance before Elijah returns. The change is a relational one. In describing his circumstances, Elijah complained that "I am the only one left." It is this particular fact that God altars before He commissions Elijah for his next season of ministry. God says to Elijah:

> Go back the way you came, and go to the Desert of Damascus. When you get there, anoint Hazael king over Aram. Also, anoint Jehu son of Nimshi king over Israel, and anoint Elisha son of Shaphat from Abel Meholah to succeed you as prophet. Jehu will put to death any who escape the sword of Hazael, and Elisha will put to death any who escape the sword of Jehu. Yet I reserve seven thousand in Israel–all whose knees have not bowed down to Baal and whose mouths have not kissed him.[133]

Elijah would not return alone. What God knows is that Elijah's confidence, faith, and persuasive power alone would never be enough to sustain him against the weight of the king's criticisms and Elijah's self-induced pressures. Elijah required help. In anticipation of Elijah's return, God commissions him with a team of people who will encourage him, defend him, partner with him, and provide him with the emotional and physical support he will need. The final act of Elijah's restoration is the

---

131 I Kings 20:10, 14
132 I Kings 20:15
133 I Kings 20:15-18

gift of new relationships. Without Hazael, Jehu, Elijah and the broader support of seven thousand faithful encouragers to join him in his future work, Elijah's would not survive. Armed with this web of support, he could now contend with the challenges before him.

Like Elijah, pastors too burn out. Some quit. Others are restored. And while pastors may hope for different circumstances in which to lead God's church or wish for the power to change those circumstances, the Christian pastor knows that the greater flow of history operates under God's jurisdiction and is His alone to control. Therefore, if clergy are to enjoy a healthy future in ministry, they must develop strategies to survive the troubling uncertainty. Just as God provided Elijah with a band of faithful supporters, God does not leave pastors without the relationships they need. God makes available to every pastor the relationships he needs, if only the pastor will seek them. It is my hope as pastors choose to seek out this team of support, they will search out as well the sustaining strength of a friend.

CHAPTER II

What is Friendship?

I wonder,
Will you be my friend? A friend
Who far beyond the feebleness of any vow or tie
Will touch the secret place where I am really I,
To know the pain of lips that plead and eyes that weep,
Who will not run away when you find me in the street
Alone and lying mangled by my quota of defeats
But will stop and stay—to tell me of another day
When I was beautiful.[1]

—James Kavanaugh

Our longing for friendship speaks to our yearning to be understood and accepted. Friends offer the hope of life amidst the mounting "quota of defeats" and light the way ahead. Like a relational "comfort food" at the banquet table of life, friends can soothe our churning fears and make the unbearable bearable once again. Friendship colorizes the landscape of our lives, for as Emerson said about friendship, "All things through thee take nobler form."[2] We instinctively know this, for we begin seeking friends as soon as we are able. We intuitively turn to them with our joys, our hurts, a good joke, a troubling question, good gossip, or a new thought. While other relationships are squeezed into our calendar of appointments, friends are welcome through an open door at nearly any time and any place. Friendship is pouring part of ourselves into another and attaching a chapter of our personal history to the person we call friend. For this reason, when we lose a close friend to distance or disagreement, we grieve it as loss.

---

[1] James Kavanaugh, *Will You Be My Friend?* (Highland Park, IL: Steven J. Nash Pub., 1990), 6.
[2] Ralph Waldo Emerson, *Collected Essays: The Complete Original First Series* (Rockville, MD: Arc Manor, 2007), 113.

We carry no deficiencies in our use the word "friend" and quite easily and intuitively know who deserve this weighty title. We need no training to know how to spot a friend. Children learn to find friends as naturally as they learn language itself. Yet despite the intuitive nature of friendship, few ever develop a careful understanding of the dynamics of this beloved relationship. Few can articulate clearly how these friendships form, what factors play into the comings and goings of our friends, and why we relate differently with some friends than we do with others. Nor do most feel the need to possess this understanding in order to enjoy friendship's benefits. Friendship happens, and that is all most need to know.

Most clergy, too, flow with friendship in much the same way, rarely giving thought to its intricacies. Yet given the precarious environment in which most pastors live and work and the therapeutic roll friendships can play in preventing burnout in ministry, it may be helpful to the pastor to grow in awareness of the nature and development of friendship in order to develop supportive friendships that may help sustain him or her through the course of ministry. If a pastor chooses to accept the importance of friendship as a key supportive relationship in pastoral ministry, then he must develop a basic understanding of what friendship is, how it is formed, how it differs from other relationships, and how friendship benefits the health and wellbeing of the people involved.

In this chapter, I seek to peel away some of the mystery from this relationship in hopes of giving clergy more precise meaning and scope to this often imprecise and complex relationship. This begins with looking at possibilities regarding a definition of friendship. What is friendship? What does it look like? Once a broad set of descriptors are in place, I will then invite into the conversation some historic voices on friendship that will demonstrate the ever changing ebb and flow of friendship and its place in culture. This will lead to the question friendship's place within the body of Christian theology, giving specific attention to friendship's restrictive nature in light of Christianity's unconditional invitation to relationship. I will, then, place friendship in its contemporary context, looking at the influence of modernity on the role of friendship today, taking particular interest in the way friendship meets the relational needs of pastors.

Friendship's Elusive Definition

When it comes to definition, defining friendship is more akin to defining light or the scent of a rose than it is anything objective or concrete. For friendship is like time. It is such a part of our everyday existence that we take little notice of it. We use it, take advantage of it, and order our day around it, but once we are asked to define it, it becomes a slippery matter that leads to more questions than answers. Consider these questions:

> Just what is friendship? What makes a relationship a *friendship* as opposed to something else? An understanding between two people? A feeling? A moral obligation? Sympathy? Love? Esteem? How does friendship differ from affection that exists between lovers, brothers, sisters, or parents and children? Or, if these are different species of friendship, what is the *genus*? Is friendship a matter of self-interest or of altruism; or something of each? Is friendship a *duty*? How does a friendship that exists for its own sake differ from one that exists for the sake of pleasure or utility? How can one tell a true friend from a false one, or friendship from flattery? Does authentic friendship exclude other people? Can friendship be jeopardized by too much intimacy?[3]

These questions capture the reality that friendship is characterized by a "fuzzy set of features."[4] Furthermore, the nature of friendship has changed through time and culture, meaning different things to different people at different stages of human history. "Friendship is a socially embedded phenomenon, and as the social fabric of a culture shifts, so does the understanding of the role and place of friendship in society."[5] One is left to wonder if any definition can really stand in the face of the relationship's genuine complexities. Yet, by attempting to attach processes and words to it, one can enter the complex world of friendships with a clearer picture of what a friend is, what a friend does, and what a friend can mean in the time of crisis.

A Unique Relationship

The reality is, friendship can more be described than defined. Whereas definition seeks the impossible task of concretizing a fluid reality, description helps us to mark the characteristics of friendship without ruling out its subjective and ever-changing nature. In thinking descriptively, a useful means of describing friendship is to compare it to other relationships. This will give space for friendship's unique qualities to emerge and will help pastors develop a more observant eye to spot the possibilities of friendship rising up among the vast sea of relationships in which pastors swim.

---

[3] Philip Blosser and Marshell Carl Bradley, eds., *Friendship: Philosophic Reflections on a Perennial Concern* (Lanham, MD: University Press of America, 1997), vii.

[4] Beverley Fehr, *Friendship Processes* (Thousand Oaks, CA: Sage Publications, 1996), 6.

[5] Gail R. O'Day, "Jesus as Friend in the Gospel of John," *Interpretation* 58, no. 2 (April 2004): 145.

First, most relationships, such as cousin or colleague or coach, are defined by the social positions that connect two people together. In contrast, friendship is a description, sometimes of a relationship already formed,[6] that describes the quality or character of that relationship. Said differently, a friendship is not defined by the position two people hold in relation to one another, but by a wide and varied list of relational characteristics two people share with one another. Thus the title of "cousin" or "colleague" or "coach" is assigned by a social position one attains in relation to others. Yet whether or not that cousin, colleague or coach can also be called a "friend" depends on certain relational qualities also being present in that relationship.

Second, friendships do not come with the social or official recognition that many other relationships do. William K. Rawlins says it this way:

> Unlike kin, it is not a certifiable blood relationship. It lacks the religious and legal warrants and the culturally sanctioned procreative function of marriage. And it is generally regarded differently from the possessive and sexual nature of romantic love. Nor is friendship objectively defined by economic contrasts as are work or professional relationships.[7]

As one sociologist writes, "In American society friendship suffers from an absence of supportive sanction."[8]

Third, friendship is different from other relationships in that friendships move beyond function to affection. A friend is "someone who likes you," as theologian Jürgen Moltmann simply put it. "You may be a respected personality, enjoy awe and admiration, and still find no one 'who likes you.'"[9] Moltmann further reminds us of the difficulty of finding this affection as we age.

---

[6] Janet Reohr, *Friendship: An Exploration of Structure and Process* (New York: Garland Publishing, Inc., 1991), ix. As Reohr states, "It is possible for two people to be friends and have no other relational connection."

[7] William K Rawlins, *Friendship Matters: Communication, Dialectics, and the Life Course* (New York: Aldine de Gruyter, 1992), 9.

[8] Janet Reohr, *Friendship: An Exploration of Structure and Process* (New York: Garland Publishing, Inc., 1991), ix.

[9] Jürgen Moltmann, "Open Friendship: Aristotelian and Christian Concepts of Friendship," in *The Changing Face of Friendship*, ed. Leroy S. Rouner, vol. 15, Boston University Studies in Philosphy and Religion (University of Notre Dame Press, 1994), 29-30. Moltmann further introduces the challenges that age brings to the development of friendship: "As children we were conscious of this world [of friendship]. But the more grown up we became, the narrower becomes our circle of friends. And there come enemies. There are competitors in the struggle for scholastic accomplishments, jobs, and careers; there are rivals in love and disappointed trust."

Fourth, friendships are usually unsought. One may be obligated to have a relationship with a "boss" or a "teacher," but the friendship relationship cannot be assigned by directive, for as sociologist Ray Pahl says, "If we feel obligated to be a friend, then it is no true friendship."[10] Certain characteristics may predict whether or not two people may become friends, yet the ultimate factors that draw two people together as friends are often more mysterious and inexplicable than predictable. One may choose to arrange a meeting between two people who have the potential for friendship, but whether or not friendship is attained is often determined by something more than a checklist of shared interests or noteworthy commonalities. In the section to follow, I will put forth particular traits that describe what many friendships contain, but this list is not a prescriptive list or one that will serve as a "formula" for creating friendship. In the end, all the ingredients that may predict friendship can be present with two people, and the glue of affection may not take hold. Emerson once captured this mysterious aspect of friendship:

> My friends have come to me unsought. The great God gave them to me. By oldest right, by the divine affinity of virtue with itself, I find them, or rather not I, but the Deity in me and in them derides and cancels the thick walls of individual character, relation, age, sex, circumstance, at which he usually connives, and now makes many one.[11]

These descriptions only begin to touch the surface of the complex nature of friendships. In fact, the astute observer will quickly observe that these descriptors are quite contemporary in nature. Not always has friendship been based in affection or been an "unsought" relationship. In other times and in other cultures, friendships have been quite utilitarian and public, in most cases decidedly male, and in the Christian context, more broadly defined to include even enemies. Definitions of friendship are fluid and reframed by each generation. Therefore, before moving further into the world of modern day friendship, it is helpful to hear the voices of the past informing us of the movement of this relationship throughout time and place.

Historic Voices on Friendship

Contemporary ideas about friendship do not arrive without a context. They are influenced by the push and pull of history and the many cultural and philosophical contributions to the nature of human friendship. It is important to add to the reservoir of meaning regarding

---

[10] Ray Pahl, *On Friendship* (Malden, MA: Polity Press, 2000), 62.
[11] Emerson, *Love & Friendship*, 38.

this special relationship by hearing those who have come before us. Nothing is exhaustive about what follows, as no serious treatment can be given to such a vast topic in such short space. Yet, it is helpful to anyone interested in understanding the inner dynamics of friendships to hear from the reflective voices of the past, for these ideas that are still speaking to us today beneath the textures of our consciousness. In the pages that follow, we look at two major influences in contemporary thinking: western and Christian thought and culture. Beginning with the Western philosophers, Aristotle will provide a window into Greek thought along with Cicero's somewhat similar perspective presenting a Roman point of view. The Christian influence will then be represented by the teachings of Jesus and the influence of a few other influential Christian writers.

Aristotle and Cicero

The broad period of time known as the classical period describes the cultural flourishing of Greek and Roman civilization that formed the basis ideals, language, art, education, and architecture of the western world. A time period thought to begin with the writings of Homer (8th-7th centuries BCE) end ending with the fall of the Roman Empire (5th century CE), this philosophical, technological, and cultural development of European culture provided a formative energy that re-emerged in the Renaissance of the 14th to 17th centuries as well as the neo-classical revival of the 18th and 19th centuries. Much of the western ideals of friendship were born in and shaped by this period.[12]

Classical definitions of friendship are often subsumed under the ancient Greek word for friendship, *philia*. The concept of friendship in the classical world was much broader and utilitarian than in the contemporary world. It is broad, in that it "takes in a much wider range of relationships than those described by the word 'friendship' in contemporary English."[13] Friendship for the ancient Greek did not quite contain the sense of "close companion" that is characteristic of friendship today. Instead, friendship "takes in family members and people we would describe as acquaintances, not friends."[14]

Friendship also took on a more utilitarian flavor in the Classical world than it does in its modern society. "Friendship may be said to depend not only on sentiments and intentions but on deeds: what counts is what one does for a friend, for that is the surest evidence of

---

[12] It is important to note that the philosophical insights from ancient Greek thinkers come to us "entirely in the masculine voice." "We know of no writings on the topic of friendship from female philosophers." Barbara Caine, ed., *Friendship: A History* (London: Equinox Publishing, 2009), 2.

[13] Caine, *Friendship: A History*, 2.

[14] Caine, *Friendship: A History*, 2.

devotion."[15] Helpfulness and service were central to the role of a friend, making the friend an ally or "one who offers help in a predicament."[16]

The social and political context of the Classical world contributed to the utilitarian nature of friendship. The ancients saw one of the city-state's primary tasks as promoting well-being among its citizens. The goal of life was to achieve *eudaimonia*, which is "most frequently translated 'happiness,' but it is more accurately translated 'human flourishing' or 'wellbeing.'"[17] Whereas in contemporary society, happiness is captured by a sense of private, subjective contentment, happiness in the ancient world was an objective state of human flourishing. Wellbeing entailed a public display of virtue that led to the achievement of "repute and lasting fame."[18] The goal of life was to flourish and to do so for the good of the society, and thus the goal friendships were to promote this flourishing. Friendships, then, "enable us to achieve human flourishing. They do this by enabling us to perform fine and noble actions. Friends are required… to assist their friends in achieving goals."[19]

This background helps to reveal why Classical Greek thinkers defined friendships in very utilitarian ways. Friendships (*philia*) came in many forms, such as the guest-friendship, collaborators, kinsmen, and political friendships.[20] All of this has led to the question of the degree to which ancient friendships mirror modern day friendships. Some have argued that the contemporary notions of friendship did not truly emerge until the Renaissance period, "or indeed still more recently, as late perhaps as the eighteenth or even nineteenth century" and that ancient friendships are more different from contemporary friendships than they are alike.[21]

Against this notion, David Konstan of Brown University argues that these differences are overstated. Because economy functions in contemporary society nearly separate and apart from one's interpersonal relationships, friendships in the modern world can function in much less utilitarian ways. Given, however, that in the ancient world, economies were "inextricably embedded in a complex of social relationships that included personal bonds," it is quite difficult to imagine ancient friendships apart from the "sordid and calculating mode of interaction."[22]

---

[15]David Konstan, *Friendship in the Classical World* (Cambridge: Cambridge University Press, 1996), 56.

[16] Konstan, *Friendship in the Classical World*, 56, 59.

[17] Caine, *Friendship: A History*, 3.

[18] Caine, *Friendship: A History*, 3.

[19] Caine, *Friendship: A History*, 5.

[20] For further reading on the nature of these friendship types, see Dirk Baltzly and Nick Eliopoulos, "Chapter One: The Classical Ideals of Friendship," in Barbara Caine, ed., *Friendship: A History* (London: Equinox Publishing, 2009), 6-12.

[21] Konstan, *Friendship in the Classical World*, 2.

[22] Konstan, *Friendship in the Classical World*, 5.

Yet this does not diminish, Kostan argues, the sense of autonomy that friendships in the classical world were able to maintain.[23]

It is against this background that Aristotle put forth his ideas on friendship. Aristotle's contribution can be best summarized by his classic differentiation of major friendship types, which reinforce Konstan's argument that friendships in the Classical period involved more than mere utility. Aristotle held that while *philia* existed in many different relationships (i.e. political, parental, marital), *philia* is unique among *philoi* (friends). When *philia* is held between friends, the friendships are often formed by one of three catalysts: utility, pleasure, or virtue.[24] To Aristotle, these functions of friendships are not the sole basis of the friendship. They do act, however, as the mechanisms for forming *philia* within friendships. In other words, "Aristotle never suggests that two people who are useful to one another are automatically and on that basis alone friends."[25] He suggests instead that while friendship may be driven ultimately by mutual affection, it is often formed by utility, pleasure, or respect for the other's virtue. The source of the *philia* will determine the duration and quality of the friendship. Friendships of pleasure, for instance, may dissolve quickly, for as Aristotle posits, "such friendships, then, are easily dissolved, if the parties do not remain like themselves; for if the one party is no longer pleasant or useful the other ceases to love him."[26]

It is the friendship of virtue that moves friendship in the Classical world beyond simply utility, or at least beyond the base utilitarian functions of pleasure and selfish need. Aristotle held that friendship held a deep moral component that begins with a deep respect for the character and virtue of the other. In this vein, the most controversial of Aristotelian ideas, perhaps, is the belief that true friendship can only truly occur among morally good people. Friendship brings out the best virtues in people as friends reflect that virtue onto one another. A friend is a "mirror of the soul," Aristotle would say.[27] Friends provide the critical "self-knowledge" that shapes moral character.[28] "Aristotle argues that being seen as the persons we are is necessary for seeing ourselves as we

---

[23] Konstan, *Friendship in the Classical World*, 6.

[24] Aristotle, *Nicomachean Ethics* (Library of Constitutional Classics, n.d.), accessed January 19, 2014, http://www.constitution.org/ari/ethic_08.htm.

[25] Konstan, *Friendship in the Classical World*, 72.

[26] Aristotle, *Nicomachean Ethics*.

[27] A phrase used by Aristotle in *Nicomachean Ethics* as quoted in Neera Kapur Badhwar, ed., *Friendship: A Philosophical Reader* (Ithaca, NY: Cornell University Press, 1993), 7.

[28] Badhwar, *Friendship: A Philosophical Reader*, 8.

are and this, in turn, is one of our deepest needs.... Friendship is particularly well-suited to fulfill this need."[29]

Because of the moral nature of the friendship relationship, Aristotle, then, saw the qualities of mutual affection and respect as fundamental to good friendships. Friendships of the highest form were held among equals, sharing the same class, education, and values.

Echoing these beliefs, Cicero was effective in passing along this understanding of friendship to the Roman world. Cicero echoed Aristotle, expanding very little upon Aristotle's ideas. [30] What Cicero did offer to the Roman world was his eloquence for language and ideas. Considered "the greatest of all Roman orators,"[31] Cicero possessed a gift of communicating the ideas of Greek and Rome to educate the masses as much as was possible.[32] Cicero echoed Aristotelian notions that friendship was a noble, and indeed moral, enterprise that could exist only between good men. The following passage from Cicero's *De Amicitia* (or *On Friendship*) demonstrates his ability to communicate with eloquence and sentiment as well as reveals his belief that friendship is most possible among equals. "In the face of a true friend a man sees as it were a second self. So that where his friend is he is; if his friend be rich, he is not poor; though he be weak, his friend's strength is his; and in his friend's life he enjoys a second life after his own is finished."[33]

Cicero's writings on friendship enabled the Aristotle's ideas to be transmitted throughout the centuries, providing a "powerful effect is shaping conceptions of friendship in the Western tradition, at least until the nineteenth century."[34] Contemporary friendship owes a debt to the thinking and writing of ancient western philosophers. Yet, the "possibility that friendship might be an open offer of love, extended even to the wicked without prior conditions, has not yet become thinkable" in the Classical world.[35] That contribution would come through the influence of Christianity, to which we now turn.

---

[29] Badhwar, *Friendship: A Philosophical Reader*, 7.

[30] Michael Pakaluk, ed., *Other Selves: Philosophers on Friendship* (Indianapolis: Hackett Pub. Co., 1991), 77. In Pakaluk's introduction to Cicero, he writes, "Cicero was not considered an original philosopher—in philosophical circles" and "is remembered today chiefly as someone who transmitted Greek philosophical thought to Roman Culture."

[31] Blosser and Bradley, *Friendship: Philosophical Reflections*, 83.

[32] Blosser and Bradley, *Friendship: Philosophical Reflections*, 83.

[33] Blosser and Bradley, *Friendship: Philosophical Reflections*, 85.

[34] Caine, *Friendship: A History*, 65–66.

[35] Liz Carmichael, *Friendship: Interpreting Christian Love* (London: T&T Clark International, 2004), 34.

Jesus and the Christian Voices

At the center of Christianity's contribution to the realm of all human relationships is the introduction of a new word into the Greek language: *agapé*.[36] Whereas *philia* was the anchor of friendship in the Classical world, *agapé* developed as a significant new term for love. *Agapé* is a love that is "wholly generous and unmotivated" and can flourish "prior to, or within, or beyond, an established relationship."[37] While much has been made in contemporary Christianity between *philia* and *agapé*, "more objective scholarship suggests that the appearance of *agapé* is to be contributed, not to theological motivation but to the natural evolution of the Greek language."[38] Liz Carmichael, in her work on Christian friendship, suggest that the language needed such a term, given that Aristotle had laid a foundation for *agapé* love in his development of the virtuous friendship. *Philia* "denoted relationship, not love itself."[39] *Agapé* "fill[ed] the gap identified by Aristotle" and provided "the capacity to name the love given by a good friend."[40]

Christianity's emphasis on *agapé* love altered yet another fundamental assumption about friendship in the Classical world. Aristotle believed that the foundation of friendship rested in mutual esteem and respect between friends. As Moltmann summarizes, "Only people who are alike can be friends. Freemen with freemen, slaves with slaves, Greeks with Greeks, barbarians with barbarians, men with men, women with women, and so forth," so "friendship in this sense means the exclusive friendship of people who are the same: *philia*."[41]

The teachings of Jesus broke through the barriers to friendship among unequals and made possible a new way of imagining loving relationships. Jesus invited his followers to engage others with love without the requirements of reciprocation or equality or common interest. In contrast to the Aristotelian belief that friendship is only possible with people who are alike, "we find the opposite picture of friendship in the New Testament: open friendship with people who are different."[42]

---

[36] Carmichael, *Friendship: Interpreting Christian Love*, 34. Carmichael writes, "*Agapé* was unknown in classical Greek and its first appearances in writing occurred in the Septuagint (LXX)."

[37] Carmichael, *Friendship: Interpreting Christian Love*, 39.

[38] Carmichael, *Friendship: Interpreting Christian Love*, 39. Carmichael gives a fuller and quite useful treatment of the natural linguistic development of *agapé* on pp. 35-39.

[39] Carmichael, *Friendship: Interpreting Christian Love*, 39.

[40] Carmichael, *Friendship: Interpreting Christian Love*, 39.

[41] Moltmann, "Open Friendship: Aristotelian and Christian Concepts of Friendship," 32.

[42] Moltmann, "Open Friendship: Aristotelian and Christian Concepts of Friendship," 32.

Moltmann argues that the foundation for a new kind of friendship is rooted in the very nature of Jesus Christ, as "King of kings, the Lord of Lords" who became "the derided Son of Man from Nazareth, 'a carpenter's son'."[43] The Christian revolution introduced great paradox to power and position. Even the symbol of the cross which the Roman Empire intended for disgrace became a sacred and idealized symbol to be admired.[44] In a move unthinkable to the ancients, it was possible to become a "friend of God."[45]

By turning the positions of power and authority upside down, the work of Jesus made a way for the new and unexpected title for the transcendent Lord: *friend.* The word "friend" is actually ascribed to Jesus only twice in the Christian scriptures, together capturing Christianity's contribution to the meaning of friendship. First, in Luke's gospel (7:34), Jesus echoes a charge laid against him that he is a "glutton and a drunkard, a friend of tax collectors and sinners." Here the issue of status and reputation is removed as a basis for friendship. Very much against the standard of the day, Jesus gained a dishonorable reputation for engaging friendships in this way. Furthermore, this is no mere object lesson of dispassionate engagement on Jesus' part. Jesus engages these less-than-respected people with joy and passion. This is no "dry sympathy, but an inviting joy in God's kingdom to those who are 'reprobates' according to the law."[46] Jesus finds an authentic respect and affection for those far outside his level of status, and the relationship now has a new commonality – their shared place in God's kingdom.[47] One may further draw that differences that prevent friendship, according to classical ideals, are of "no theological significance," for "in the eyes of God, human beings are equally worthy of his loving kindness."[48] In the end, Jesus does not so much as reverse Aristotle's notion that friendship is based in mutual affection as he does to demonstrate how widely mutual affection can be practiced and how broad friendship can be.

The second use of "friend" as ascribed to Jesus emerges in John's gospel (15:13-14): "Greater love has no one than this: to lay down one's life for one's friends. You are my friends if you do what I command." In

---

[43] Moltmann, "Open Friendship: Aristotelian and Christian Concepts of Friendship," 33.

[44] Moltmann, "Open Friendship: Aristotelian and Christian Concepts of Friendship," 33.

[45] Mark Vernon, *The Meaning of Friendship* (New York: Palgrave Macmillan, 2010), 128-129. Vernon adds, "Aristotle argued that one could no more be friends with a god than one could with a king: both are superior to mere mortals, and friendship flounders when the would-be friends are unequal in status, power and capacities."

[46] Moltmann, "Open Friendship" 34.

[47] Moltmann, "Open Friendship" 34.

[48] Carmichael, *Friendship: Interpreting Christian Love*, 284.

this text, being "friend with God" takes on a much less sentimental flavor and moves deeply into a sense of sacrifice. Theological and practical implications are involved in such an idea. Theologically, Jesus opens the possibility not only that friendship is possible among "unequals," but that a friendship with God is also possible. The power distance between God and his people is no longer a barrier to connection with God. "In the fellowship of Jesus they no longer experience God as Lord, nor only as Father; rather they experience him in his innermost nature as Friend."[49]

Beyond the theological contributions of this text come the practical ones, rooted in the simple idea that "Jesus does not merely talk the language of friendship; he lives out his life and death as a friend."[50] Classical philosophy held out that death for a friend as the highest act of friendship. By moving this from an ideal to a reality, Jesus demonstrated the true depths of friendship, as specifically demonstrated by God through Jesus Christ. The real act of Jesus' sacrificial death for his friends enables trust and depth of love to be felt and experienced by those who recognize God's friendship. Furthermore, the implications for the Christian community and the depth of relationship available to them are offered in Jesus through his words, "Love each other as I have loved you."[51] Jesus, through a re-imagined definition and experience of friendship, offers the possibility of a depth of relationship that perhaps had never been imagined before: a joyful relationship among unequals that extends to the depths of the greatest self-sacrifice. "God in Christ extended friendship to all human beings, and to be a 'friend of sinners', hitherto a genuine insult or impossible paradox, now becomes thinkable and possible."[52]

The seeds of this new way of looking at relationship provided much raw material for the development of Christian friendship over the centuries to come. Numerous Christian philosophers and leaders, such as Ambrose of Milan, John Chrysostom, Aelred of Rievaulx, Thomas Aquinas, Soren Kierkegaard, and C.S. Lewis—to name a few—wrestled with where the traditionally exclusive and secretive nature of intimate friendship rested within the value of Christianity's brotherly love for all persons. Of these significant thinkers and theologians, St. Augustine is helpful as a means of merging the work of Jesus Christ with the contributions of the classical writers.

Augustine, offering what has been argued as "the most sophisticated reflection on friendship" in the Christian tradition[53] brings a theological

---

[49] Moltmann, "Open Friendship," 35.
[50] O'Day, "Jesus as Friend in the Gospel of John," 151.
[51] O'Day, "Jesus as Friend in the Gospel of John," 151.
[52] Carmichael, *Friendship: Interpreting Christian Love*, 39.
[53] Caine, *Friendship: A History*, 81.

element to friendship that moves the relationship beyond what Aristotle and Cicero imagined. In contrast to Aristotle, who posited a friendship (albeit less than ideal) based on need, and Cicero, who held that "true friendship was offered for the sake of the other," Augustine believed that true friendship was offered for the sake of God.[54] This concept flowed out of both Augustine's personal awareness of his own sinfulness and need to make God the supreme focus of his life as well as his struggle to bring together the beauty and virtue of friendship with its self-beneficial aspects.

Augustine affirmed a seemingly contradictory belief that good friendship involved both a love of self and a profound love of God. Self-love, despite its clear conflicts with Christian thinking, is necessary to friendship, for friendships cannot be entered into deeply, openly and freely until the persons involved first befriend themselves. But to make the friendship a means of showing devoted love to God

Augustine's reflections on friendship bring into a fuller view the struggle that Christian thinkers throughout the ages have faced in regards to the friendship relationship. Augustine, for example, grieved intensely the loss of a close friend, only years later to lament that his love for his friend may have exceeded his love for God.[55] Can relationships that serve us so deeply and function so exclusively be reconciled with the true nature of *agapé* love as expressed in Jesus Christ? Does a true friendship rooted in the Christian virtue of *agapé* look so different than other traditional friendship to make them another kind of relationship entirely?

Early Christian thinkers generally resolved this by acknowledging a "two-tier system" that included a general love for all humankind rooted in the *agapé* love of Jesus Christ and the more specific, affectionate and bonding love of friends.[56] In fact, many of these early Christian writers "reveal their belief that the exclusive, mutual love [of friendship] is superior to the general love [of humankind]."[57] For Augustine, for instance, this kind of exclusive love became a way for him to understand the second part of the divine commandment to "love your neighbor as yourself."[58]

Not all Christian theologians and writers would become so comfortable with such a distinction. The Christian philosopher, Søren Kierkegaard, presents the ultimate challenge to friendship based on his

---

[54] Caine, *Friendship: A History*, 81.

[55] Carolinne White, *Christian Friendship in the Fourth Century* (Cambridge: Cambridge University Press, 2002), 186.

[56] White, *Christian Friendship in the Fourth Century*, 219.

[57] White, *Christian Friendship in the Fourth Century*, 219.

[58] White, *Christian Friendship in the Fourth Century*, 219.

understanding of Christian theology.[59] Kierkegaard was critical of any relationship based on self-love and could only see friendship in direct contrast to "neighbor-love," which he held was at the root of Christian love. Seeing friendship as kin to erotic love in its feelings and spontaneous affections, he sees in friendship a tendency towards pride, self-congratulation, and narcissism. For he counted friendship among the relationships of "poetic love," for it is a relationship that is "partial and transient," emerging out of a love of "mood and inclination."[60] To embrace relationships that are different than neighbor-love, Kierkegaard wonders how virtuous any such relationship can be, since it is characterized by something other than self-renunciation and unconditionality. If true Christian relationship is based on equality, arising out of our equality before God, how can one embrace a "friend" with a special love and exclusivity and deem that relationship as consistent with being Christian? As Kierkegaard himself says, "Christianity has misgivings about erotic love and friendship because preference in passion or passionate preference is really another form of self-love.[61] Kierkegaard cannot resolve the issue. As Mark Vernon writes, "Kierkegaard does his best to bury friendship."[62]

The contemporary Catholic thinker and writer, Paul Wadell, argues in his book, *Friendship and the Moral Life*, that Kierkegaard pits friendship against *agape* rather than root both in "the God in whom love is revealed."[63] Wadell continues,

> The weakness in Kierkegaard's earlier analysis was failing to see that philia and agape share the same criterion insofar as both are genuinely love to the degree they are modeled on God. Once it is acknowledged that both Christian friendship and agape originate in the same love, not only are the reconcilable, they are also inseparable; that is, we not only know why agape is not opposed to friendship, we also know why it is friendship's most perfect expression.[64].

Friendship, for Wadell, is the relationship in which agape love can be learned. If one learns to love and care for a friend, entirely for his or her own sake, then agape love, learned within the safety of friendship, can

---

[59] Vernon, *The Meaning of Friendship*, 130. Vernon reminds us that Kierkegaard "once wrote to make life more difficult for people," noting his surname means "graveyard."

[60] Pakaluk, *Other Selves*, 233.

[61] From Kierkegaard, *Works of Love*, as reproduced in Pakaluk, *Other Selves*, 240.

[62] Vernon, *The Meaning of Friendship*, 130.

[63] Paul J. Wadell, *Friendship and the Moral Life* (Notre Dame: University of Notre Dame Press, 1989), 83.

[64] Wadell, *Friendship and the Moral Life*, 83.

then flow to others and to enemies.[65] Furthermore, it appears that Kierkegaard's trouble with friendship rises out of his focus on the different natures of the friendship versus Christian love of others. Because friendship is between two who are attracted together in preferential love, the relationship by its very nature is born out of a corrupt basis and remains helplessly so, Wadell redirects attention away from the characters within loving relationships (i.e., friends, others, enemies), but in the place of God in the relationship. The hope of Christian love in any relationship is "not that [the relationship] be non-preferential, but that its source, center, and aim be God."[66] One could imagine that even "selfless love for others" can be rooted in corrupt motives, by mere obligation, or legalistic pressures, and thus be rooted in something other than God. Whereas, friendships formed out of preference and reciprocation can flower into true expressions of Godly love. As Wadell puts it, "By preferring God, the friends learn what it means to prefer one another. Thus a mistaken love is not a preferential love, but one exclusive of God."[67]

Another counterpoint to Kierkegaard's "either-or" posture on friendship is found in the work of C.S. Lewis. Lewis offers a way to embrace friendship not only as acceptable within the framework of Christian values, but as a high mark in Christian living worth seeking and achieving. In his work, *The Four Loves*, Lewis notes that friendship is a unique and "spiritual"[68] relationship because it is the one most "unnecessary" and most freely entered into for its own value.[69] Lewis eloquently raises the value of friendship as a high form of Christian love, for "[t]his love, free from instinct, free from all duties but those which love has freely assumed, almost wholly free from jealousy, and free without qualification from the need to be needed, is eminently spiritual. It is the sort of love one can imagine between angels."[70] Friendship, he argues, is utilitarian only in that friends would not be friends if they did not meet needs in one another as they arose, but in essence, "Friendship is utterly free from Affection's need to be needed."[71] Instead, friends stand alongside one another and see the world together, both sharing a

---

[65] Wadell, *Friendship and the Moral Life*, 81. Wadell states, "In this way, agape and philia are not mutually exclusive, they are intrinsically connected: friendship is the love in which agape is learned."

[66] Wadell, *Friendship and the Moral Life*, 82.

[67] Wadell, *Friendship and the Moral Life*, 83–84.

[68] C. S. Lewis, *The Four Loves* (New York: Harcourt Brace Jovanovich, 1991), 77.

[69] Lewis, *The Four Loves*, 71.

[70] Lewis, *The Four Loves*, 77.

[71] Lewis, *The Four Loves*, 69.

common journey, a love of truth, and affection for questions of great importance, for "Friendship must be about something."[72]

One quickly gets the sense that Lewis' reflections are far more personal than theological. He writes more poetically than analytically. Liz Carmichael also points out that Lewis' reflections on friendship are "rooted in the kind of donnish companionship, redolent of pubs, pipe-smoke and walking holidays, that he himself enjoyed."[73] However, Lewis is helpful to the contemporary pastor, living under the weight of the reality that human beings are rarely able to devote the kind of analytical muscle to human relationships that the Augustines and Kierkegaards can afford. Lewis provides a practical embrace of friendship that both admits to its limitations and potential narcissistic hazards as well as embraces its high spiritual value. There is a sense of reality to Lewis that corresponds with the everyday challenges of pastors who hold up and seek to lead others into unconditional "neighbor-love," but who also live with the desire for a close and intimate relationship that touches a place that neighbor-love cannot always reach.

The history of friendship is complex and extensive, with the vast expanse of time and culture, faith and philosophy all making their distinguishing marks. In this chapter, we have had the space only to observe only two main sets of cultural, theological, and philosophical voices – the Greek and Christian voices – in seeking to understand the primary historic influences on our practice of friendship today. While there is much more left unsaid than a complete history would allow, these powerful voices are most relevant the practice of pastors in friendship in the 21st century. Yet these historic influences are only part of the story. Modern friendship may have its roots in Greek and Christian thought, but it is the powerful forces of contemporary culture and modern life that have made friendship not only a crucial element to meaningful living, but also a formidable challenge to develop and maintain. To these cultural forces of modern life we now turn.

Friendship in the Contemporary World

When flowing into the contemporary context, the waters of friendship muddy significantly. Contemporary life, with its constant change, remarkable expansion of communication, and increasing urbanization, mobilization, and digitization, introduces even greater complexity into the world of friendships. In previous eras, one could rely on a rather consistent cultural, social, and philosophical environment to form the backdrop to friendship formation and development. Place

---

[72] Lewis, *The Four Loves*, 66.
[73] Carmichael, *Friendship: Interpreting Christian Love*, 155.

friendship into the modern context with all its rapidly forming social and cultural complexities, and you have and even greater set of ambiguous features to apply to the friendship relationship.

The complexity begins with the simple question of how moderns use the word "friend." The "wide range of close informal relationships" to which the term friendship is so liberally applied[74] contributes to the murkiness of today's friendships. It is not unusual for the term "friend" to be applied to a new acquaintance "friended" in an online social network. Yet another may apply the term strictly, meaning the one(s) with whom they have a "second self." In the post-modern context, those two wide-ranging definitions might be used unquestionably by the same person. One sociologist termed it, "the irreducibility of friendship,"[75] noting that the wide range of experiences people attach to friendship and the relative nature of the relationship means that the concept of friendship is tested not against an agreed-upon definition or guiding philosophy, but against one's subjective, personal experience with friendship. Hence the unsettling ambiguity.

The fears about the effects of modernity on friendship have been present from the beginning. Twentieth century German sociologist, Georg Simmel, suggested that modernity would redefine friendship negatively. He and other sociologists predicted that as the industrialization of society progressed, social relationships would fall prey to the inevitable "commodification."[76] It was feared that capitalistic society would require that friendships be formed on the basis of its mutual benefits, measured by the ability of friends to reward one another. As Ray Pahl describes, "The assumption appeared to be that people were slippery little tricksters endlessly engaged in games of one-upmanship with each other."[77] The free economy required the beneficence of alliances and a collection of "friends" who would amount to little more than "advisors, associates, and backers" who "would not necessarily have any specific ties of affection."[78]

Yet despite these pessimistic predictions, friendship manages to find life in the modern era. Friendship may be riding along in a wave of turbulent cultural forces, but the nature of friendship has been and continues to be formed and re-formed to fit the shape of contemporary culture. Friendship has found a way to navigate through the challenges of class distinctions, gender differences, and cultural movements. It has survived and begs for further definition in light of societal changes of

---

[74] Pahl, *On Friendship*, 1.
[75] Vernon, *The Meaning of Friendship*, 9.
[76] Pahl, *On Friendship*, 36.
[77] Pahl, *On Friendship*, 50.
[78] Pahl, *On Friendship*, 53.

recent eras. Therefore, an additional set of descriptors can now be offered as a means of setting the context for friendship today. What follows is a set of observations gleaned from the latest in contemporary thought on the subject of friendship. There is no particular order to these descriptors, nor is it intended to be an exhaustive list. It simply seeks to describe some ways in which friendship is unique to its current context and begins to identify how these might challenge the pastor in friendship formation. These challenges will lay groundwork for the research in upcoming chapters as pastors speaks to effects of these challenges in their ability to form meaningful and helpful friendships.

Differentiated Friendships

First, friendship is highly contextualized, and some might say "differentiated," in the contemporary world. Given the fragmentation and categorization of the modern lifestyle, it is not uncommon for moderns to develop different friends for different "categories" of their lives. Work friends, recreational friends, church friends, rotary club friends – one may have different friends for different areas of life.[79] For modernity itself divides and splits life into categories and specialized roles, making it difficult in the modern world for one to have "holistic" friendships. Mobility and education influence this as well. Different life-stages may generate a distinctive set of friends for different eras of one's life. "Some of these fall away as we go through life; others are remembered at Christmas or perhaps at birthdays, and yet others are maintained with some effort through visits, letters, telephone calls, and now email."[80]

Pastors too are pressed into such categorization as they develop a variety of different friendship types, such as seminary friends, collegial friends, congregational friends, friends from past congregations, neighborhood friends. Each category has its own implications for how the pastor enters into those relationships. "Old friends" may be a comforting and rejuvenating force. "Congregational friends" may bring anxiety or role confusion or an even higher set of expectations for the pastor. To be sure, the compartmentalization of contemporary life means that all friends are not equal for the pastor and that understanding and discernment are crucial.

Friends as Surrogate Family

A second aspect of friendship unique to modern day society is the use of friends as surrogate family. It was once a rigid principle that

---

[79] Pahl, On Friendship, 14.
[80] Pahl, On Friendship, 14.

friends and family are significantly different relationships, for one is chosen, and the other is chosen for you. As part of our mobile society, friendship often replaces family as a means of primary social support. More and more people leave the bonds of family necessitated by geographical separation in search of a new "social convoy."[81] Pahl suggests that friendships are "taking over various social tasks, duties, and functions, from family and kin."[82] One group of researchers observe that "family relationships came in a distant third" to romantic relationships and friends when people were asked to identify their closest, most supportive relationships.[83]

Pastors are often at the mercy of continuous mobilization throughout their career, given how often pastors relocate to serve a new calling. While other professionals may transition in their job, they are not always required to leave their town, leave their church, and leave their friends to do so. For the pastor, the transition most often means not only a change of workplace, but the loss of all social support the pastor has worked so hard to develop. And because dislocation is built into the fabric of pastoral life, pastors rarely have a large network of extended family in close proximity to provide support in coping with such change. Pastors too long for family-like support and, as is now common in the culture, they seek a surrogate family through their friends. Given the premise put forth thus far that friendship formation is an especially difficult challenge for pastors, one begins to see more clearly why loneliness is such a significant part of the pastor's reported experience.

Family as Friends

A third observation is that contemporary society reframes the concept of family as friends. There may be today a greater possibility to consider a family member a "close friend" since the patriarchal and hierarchical lines dividing family in traditional societal structures have largely been blurred, if not erased.[84] Given that dependence upon family is less critical to survival than in times past, the luxury exists for family members to choose to function as friends as the ties bound by necessity fade. Thus, the value of particular family members is often judged by the degree to which those family members are considered friends.

Given the isolation pastors may experience as a result of regular mobilization and the difficulties around the formation of genuine friendships, it is not uncommon for the full weight of emotional and

---

[81] Pahl, *On Friendship*, 9.
[82] Pahl, *On Friendship*, 8.
[83] Fehr, *Friendship Processes*, 3.
[84] Pahl, *On Friendship*, 35–36.

relational support to fall on the pastor's spouse. One can imagine the pressures placed on the marriage of a pastor without friend support, as the pastor's spouse becomes the sole tend of the pastor's emotional and relational needs.

Gender Influences in Friendship

A fourth development in contemporary life is the influence of gender equality on the nature of friendships. In much of the span of the history of friendships, one fundamentally held assumption was that "friendship was possible only between men."[85] Because many a philosopher believed that only men were capable of living virtuous lives in the ancient world, it followed that friendship was a relationship only enjoyable by men.[86] However, as cultural changes of modernization swept through the 19th and 20th centuries, not only did women come to enjoy the benefits of friendship, but friendships among women came to be seen as "more sincere, more meaningful and more significant than those of men."[87] Women began to discover that their own sense of "who they are and where they are going" was more likely to be found in close friendships with other women.[88] Finding a marriage partner did not mean the end of friendship for women, and in fact may be strengthen friendship, as women felt more comfortable exploring issues of marriage and motherhood with other women than with their husbands.[89] Therefore, as friendships came to take on a more emotional aspect in the 19th and 20th centuries and found support through the women's movement of the 1970's and 80's, the modern era became the "age of female friendship, or perhaps the age when friendship became female."[90]

If friendship is trending as more highly developed in women than in men, one begins to wonder how this affects those faith traditions in which the clergy are predominately male. Has this trend added just one more cultural barrier to the work that male clergy have to do to form meaningful friendships? Furthermore, what is the challenge for female clergy who may be more inclined to enter more deeply into intimate friendship and lean more heavily on a friend for support, but may be following a long history of male leadership where congregational friendships were considered off limits by the clergy? There are more questions than answers here, but the questions are important ones to

---

[85] Caine, *Friendship: A History*, xii.
[86] Caine, *Friendship: A History*, xii.
[87] Caine, *Friendship: A History*, xii.
[88] Pahl, *On Friendship*, 37.
[89] Pahl, *On Friendship*, 37.
[90] Caine, *Friendship: A History*, 281.

consider as pastors seek to overcome challenges to meaningful friendships.

Friendship as Free From Obligation

One aspect of contemporary friendship is the idea that friendships ought to be free from the normal social roles and obligations that create binds in many other kinds of relationships. "Friendship, as a continuous creation of personal will and choice, is ungoverned by the structural definitions that bear on family and kinship."[91] While some expectations do exist in friendships, most of that obligation is in the range of emotional support and advice-giving. Even in these cases, friends have often shown reluctance to place such burdens on the friendship, for fear of "put[ting] the ideal of friendship to the test."[92] The ideal contemporary friendships exist for the sake of themselves rather than for political or obligatory reasons of ages past.

The effects of this reality on pastors will be explored in more detail in the next chapter. The word here is simply that pastors must navigate through the reality that friendships formed in the context of congregational life are rarely the kind that leave behind social obligation or expectations. The pastor's congregant who becomes her friend still retains a series of expectations of the pastor. While the pastor may desire to escape her role in the presence of a congregational friend, the likelihood is that this never can fully be. If pastoral expectations fail to be met in some way, the supportive friendship now is in jeopardy of becoming a relationship crisis for the pastor. It appears that pastors may struggle to enjoy the luxury of friendships unencumbered by public role (of congregational pastor) or obligation (to pastor the friend/congregant when in need). Certainly there are implications to consider as the pastor weighs the benefits and disadvantages of close, congregational friends. The pastor certainly has more at risk when expectations are intertwined with friendship.

Friendship as Secretive

A fifth quality of friendship shaped by contemporary life is the secrecy now common to friendships. Friendships had greater opportunity to flourish in an increasingly urbanized society, since the city allowed for such privacy to develop in a way village life—which allowed no secrets—could not.[93] As people moved deeper into their urbanized societies, the value of secrecy with trusted friends increased. This trend only continues

---

91 Pahl, *On Friendship*, 38.
92 Pahl, *On Friendship*, 38.
93 Caine, *Friendship: A History*, 282.

with increased communication and the advancement of social media. Life is moving further out into the open, making areas once consider private to be available for public consumption. This trend towards openness has not eliminated secrecy from contemporary life, but, it could be argued, has deepens the need for secrecy among trusted friends. Secrecy and friendship will likely continue to be linked closely together as these trends continue.

One can imagine the feelings congregation members might experience if the assumption of secrecy in friendship is projected onto the relationship between a pastor and his or her friends. The pastor is expected to be a "friend to all" and "impartial" in affection for the congregation. To have a friend is to have someone who holds your secrets, which may be perceived as inequitable care by the congregation. This puts the pastor in a challenging spot, choosing either to abandon meaningful friendships within the congregation or to keep those friendships secret from the congregation and risk a perception of further secrecy or underhandedness.

Friendship and Social Media

Lastly, one cannot avoid the influence that social media and the electronic connectedness has had on the landscape of friendship. Historically, proximity was a significant environmental factor in the formation of friendships.[94] While online interaction may never replace physical proximity as the "first step" of friendship formation, certainly the nature of the friendship and its cultivation will be influenced by online interaction in a way that is still unfolding. It was first feared that virtual communities would replace traditional face-to-face interaction. One hopeful sign is that "there has not been a mass retreat from face-to-face sociability, and it seems that the Internet is mainly used to complement and sustain existing relationships rather than creating entirely new personal networks."[95] The digital revolution is still unfolding, however, and friendships may be in the process of being reshaped to fit the profound presence of social media in contemporary life.

Pastors, likewise, are on the front end of fully understanding the impact of social networks and media on the inner workings of ministry life. This impact is perhaps just as profound on the way pastors choose to relate personally to people who they call friends. As with many sudden developments, benefits and disadvantages are immediately identifiable. The benefit of social media is the ability of the pastor to reach out to

---

[94] Fehr, *Friendship Processes*, 44.

[95] Liz Spencer and Ray Pahl, *Rethinking Friendship: Hidden Solidarities Today* (Princeton, NJ: Princeton University Press, 2006), 24.

supportive relationships and friendships that were once limited by geographical barriers. The pastor in need of companionship is now within electronic reach of close friends who may be miles or continents apart. On the other hand, if the pastor defers to social media as his or her primary source of interpersonal support, the pastor will quickly reach the limits what online relationships can provide. Social media may help the pastor feel a greater sense of connection to people past and present, far and near, but it may also become a deterrent to the necessary work of developing interpersonal, face-to-face bonds that can be so healing.

Friendship and Pastoral Life

Now that some challenges have been identified as pastors engage the issue of friendship in its modern context, it is important to begin identifying what particular needs exist in the life of the pastor that could be met through rich and meaningful friendships. The particulars of this will be fleshed out in the research outlined in the coming chapters as pastors in the field identify ways in which friendships have helped them meet spiritual, emotional, and relational needs in them. Meanwhile, a few ideas can help to germinate the thought process about where the pastor's need and the pastor's friendships can meet in a healthy and healing way.

Need for Affirmation and Affection

In considering the needs of a pastor, we return to the words of Jurgen Moltmann who suggests at the core, a friend is "someone who likes you." Pastors function in challenging times where the "role" of pastor and spiritual caregiver may sometimes lead to attacks on the position (i.e. "The pastor is leading the church in the wrong direction."). Under the duress of continued stress, the attacks on the position may easily feel like attacks on the person. Furthermore, the pastor may feel disenfranchised by his or her broader community due to the growing negative associations that some outside the religious world place on clergy in general. These affronts to one's title and role may feel like rejection at a deep and base level of being. The feelings of isolation that result and the perceived challenge to one's personhood can leave the pastor feeling wounded and needy. Certainly, a friend who "likes you" can serve as a check to those feelings by placing a new dialogue in the mind: that those who know me like me.

The Need for Mutuality

The benefit of friendship for the pastor is not simply on the receiving end. Friendship also provides an outlet for a healthy balance of relational giving and receiving. Pastors, as a profession, tend to struggle with compassion fatigue from the continual outpouring of energy into the needs of people around them. Often this expenditure of energy is unidirectional, leaving the pastor in a continual state of giving without much in return. A healthy friendship can provide a meaningful and reciprocal relationship based in mutuality. Mutuality in friendship creates a bi-directional flow of giving and taking that is far more balanced than is experienced in the everyday world of ministry. This healthy relationship can be a healing contrast to the continual relational sacrifice that often at the center of pastor/parishioner relationships.

The Need for Unconditional Acceptance

Another benefit of friendship that can bolster the pastor in troubled times is the unconditional nature of close friendships. As will be explored in the chapters to come, relationships in the congregational setting have an economy to them. The pastor's acceptance among congregants is at times conditional to the results that he or she can produce. While this may not be an intentional or conscious attitude among congregants, given the personal nature of ministry and the deeply spiritual places the pastor's ministry touches in people, when situations develop that threaten the spiritual and emotional stability of some parishioners, a natural relational distance with the pastor may then occur. Pastors who enter a season of declining attendance or stumble upon a conflict-producing issue or make an unpopular leadership decision may soon discover that people they once perceived as loyal and unconditional are now distanced from the pastor by the issue(s) at hand. The experience of conditionality in relationships during troubled times can churn feelings of abandonment and disloyalty, producing a sense of vulnerability in the pastor that, if not attended to, can lead to a spiral of increasingly toxic relationships.

To have within one's close circle of support a set of friends who can stand unconditionally with the pastor in a way that reminds the pastor of his or her personal worth can act as a check against the threatening and personal feelings the pastor may experience. When nurtured by healthy, unconditional relationships, the pastor may then be able to recalibrate his or her emotions and assumptions and see more clearly the needs of hurting (and sometimes toxic) people rather than reacting out of hurt in a way that is often unproductive. By having his or her needs for unconditional relationships met, the pastor may be better able to manage his or her anxiety in a way that fosters intentionality rather than reactivity in meeting the needs of the congregation.

The Need for Relief from Role Expectations

Returning to a significant need of the pastor as identified in chapter one, we name once again the importance of the pastor to be able to step out of role. No one can serve, even with the best of intentions, in a 24-

hour a day, seven-day a week role without stepping out of that role from time to time for the sake of relief from accompanying expectations. A friend who can relationally transcend the pastor's function as pastor gives the pastor a place of normalcy outside the rush and pace of day-to-day ministry. Friends remind the pastor of who they are independent of their role. Friends engage the fuller scope of the pastor's personhood, touching the "hidden" areas of a pastor's personal life that the congregation may never see or appreciate. A friend can appreciate the pastor's sense of humor or her personality quirks or his short-temperedness without feeling the role of pastor suffers because of it. While some congregation members might interpret the pastor's "humanity" as a personal shortcoming, a friend sees no disingenuousness or incongruity. The friend does what a congregation member may struggle to do—to honor the whole person of the pastor through understanding and acceptance.

The intent of these beginning chapters has been to set the table for the challenge that pastors face in regards to friendship and congregational life. Pastors have a deep need for the "utility" of friendships for all the reasons stated above. Yet pastors are expected to represent before their congregants the unconditional nature of relationships that Jesus espoused. While friendships can be a source of hope and healing, they can also bring about theological and practical conflict for the pastor as he or she models the faith for others. How pastors navigate these tricky waters and absorb the fruit of this relational gift into their lives is an ongoing challenge. In the chapters to follow, the research will move from the scholastic to the observable. We will look at how particular pastors in today's context of ministry have dealt with these challenges in their pastoral leadership. We will look not only for what has worked and what has not, but will look also for helpful patterns that, once extracted from the experience of today's pastors, can be applied to the variety of contexts that pastors serve.

CHAPTER III

Friendships Inside the Church

After some time Paul said to Barnabas,
"Let's go back and visit each city where we previously preached
the word of the Lord, to see how the new believers are doing."
Barnabas agreed and wanted to take along John Mark.
But Paul disagreed strongly....
Their disagreement was so sharp that they separated.
—Acts 15: 36-39 (NLT)

And Jonathan made David reaffirm his vow of friendship again,
for Jonathan loved David as he loved himself.
—I Samuel 20: 17 (NLT)

While few things are more joyful than true kinship, little is more heartbreaking than broken friendship. We cherish those David/Jonathan moments, but always at the risk of the Paul/Barnabas experience. When the pastor invests in the deep and complex world of pastoral relationships, the pastor opens himself up to the reality of a range of relational experiences—some that nurture the soul, and others that inflict painful relational distress.

The Paul/Barnabas story is stark in its honesty and a surprise to any reader who understands the divine and historic influence of Paul, the Apostle of Jesus Christ. Embedded in the story of the emergence of the Christian faith—an emergence fueled by the passion and wisdom of Paul—is a cautionary, if not foreboding tale. The intimate-friendship-turned-fractured-relationship of Paul and Barnabas sobers any pollyannish tendencies a pastor may have around the belief that "good Christians" never encounter relationship troubles. In fact, their story sets the tone for a look at the intricacies of the pastor and his or her friendships inside the church.

Paul and Barnabas

Luke, the gospel writer, in describing the work of the apostles, details the radical transformation of Saul, the Christian-hunter, determined to eliminate this new and dangerous threat to the stability of long-held Jewish traditions. After a season of persecution against followers of "The Way," Saul's own way was literally disrupted by a supernatural Christ encounter that left him blind, humbled, and radically transformed. Arising from the brokenness of his experience, Saul would eventually set aside his Jewish name to embrace the Roman citizenship captured in the name, Paul, in order to infuse the Good News into the Roman world and beyond.

Yet Paul's early passion quickly hit a road block. When Paul arrived in Jerusalem, "he tried to join the disciples, but they were afraid of him, not believing he really was a disciple."[1] His past efforts against the Christians were fresh in the minds of all those touched by his persecution. Caught between his newfound zeal and the disciples' mistrust, Paul found an advocate in Barnabas. Testifying about Paul's transformative experience and his recent ministry in Damascus, Barnabas facilitated a much-needed trust among the Christ-followers that enabled Paul to set off on his new calling to "speak boldly in the name of Jesus."[2]

The bond between Paul and Barnabas seems almost brotherly as together they confronted false teachers,[3] channeled monetary assistance to needy believers,[4] spent a year instructing new Christ-followers,[5] preached to Gentiles,[6] received the blessing of the Holy Spirit,[7] and risked their lives "for the name of our Lord Jesus Christ."[8] Such a relationship must have served as a profound comfort to Paul, who continuously faced struggle and opposition. Certainly the presence of Barnabas, his original defender and continuous ministry companion, functioned as much-needed encouragement to Paul. Even the early apostles recognized Barnabas' encouraging nature, choosing to call him not by his Cyprian name, Joseph, but by the name Barnabas, which means "Son of Encouragement."[9] Luke says of his character, "He was a good man, full

---

[1] Acts 9:26.
[2] Acts 9:28.
[3] Acts 13:4-12.
[4] Acts 11:27-30.
[5] Acts 11:25-26.
[6] Galatians 2:1-2, 9.
[7] Acts 13:2.
[8] Acts 15:25-26.
[9] Acts 4:36.

of the Holy Spirit and faith, and a great number of people were brought to the Lord."[10]

It is with the bonds of this relationship in mind that the reader is confronted by an agonizing turn in their relationship. In a decision over whether or not to include John Mark in a missionary journey to encourage believers in the churches they had helped to found, Paul and Barnabas engaged in a "sharp disagreement" of such intensity that "they parted company."[11] These terse words are shocking in their brevity, for nothing further is said to explain how such a long and meaningful relationship could fracture so quickly in the face of a seemingly narrow debate. The only clue to the depth of the division comes in Paul's letter to the Galatians when he describes the "Son of Encouragement" as one who was "carried away" by "hypocrisy."[12]

It would certainly be helpful to know more about what other factors may have been behind this division. Was Paul revealing a hyper-sensitivity in his own character by reacting so sharply against John Mark's earlier act of disloyalty? Was Barnabas reacting against Paul's calm rationality out of an emotionally clouded defense of a family member? Was their disagreement hasty and short-sighted? Was it necessary? Does the productivity of their separate ministries soften the blow of the reader's disappointment? Any answers are speculative.

What is without speculation is this: a disagreement about a particular process of ministry resulted in a fractured friendship—one that until this point had served both Paul and Barnabas to bolster them in the face of vast hardship and opposition. Two men who seemed to balance each other with complementary gifts and skills found that they could no longer serve effectively together. Whether the division arose out of defense of high principles or simply revealed some deeper personal weaknesses of two men's human condition, the textured and ugly reality of this incident reminds us that even among great men of Christian history, conflict happens. Friendships fracture. Ministry complexities can sabotage what appear to be healthy relationships.

The Context of Congregational Life

One thing contemporary pastors share with Paul and Barnabas is the depth of relationship within Christian community. In the church there exists the high standard of *koinonia*. *Koinonia* is the deep communion of fellowship that is at the heart of Christian discipleship.[13] In the context of

---

[10] Acts 11:24.

[11] Acts 15:39.

[12] Galatians 2:13.

[13] John R. W Stott, *The Message of Acts: The Spirit, the Church & the World*, The Bible Speaks Today (Leicester, England; Downers Grove, IL: Inter-Varsity Press, 1994), 83.

the *ecclesia*, Christian relationships develop a deeper, spiritual significance that produces wonderfully rich and deeply held connections that (Christians may argue) in their ideal form exceed the richness of relationships found in a secular or non-Christian environment.

Even without attaching any theological or spiritual meaning to Christian relationships to set them apart from other relationships, one could argue that the insular nature of the church life alone intensifies relationships in the church more powerfully than in society at large. Thus, Christian relationships are deepened not only by a theological ideal of *koinonia*, but are compounded by the natural social bonding of community life within the church. And certainly this is true for the busy pastor who finds most every aspect of his or her life–vocational, social, spiritual–deeply entwined in the world of congregational life.

Given the many connecting factors that form deep and spiritual relationships in the church, it is no surprise that along with the positive side of Christian relationships, there are also deep hurts and disappointments when those relationships fail. The same environment that produces deep and meaningful *koinonia* can produce the greatest disappointments too. When intensely formed relationships experience the collateral damage of church conflict or the messiness of role confusion or the painful inevitabilities of pastoral transition, the woundedness that results can be just as profound.

It is no surprise, then, that some of the prevailing wisdom handed down to the ministers in training often exists in the form of prohibition and warning. Pastors should never be friends with their congregants, young pastors are told. The student pastor is advised to maintain a "professional distance" with his or her parishioners to mitigate the risks associated with getting "too close."

Is this good advice or an over-reaction? Is it even possible for pastors to completely insulate or "professionalize" their congregational relationships enough to avoid the messy complications of pastoral relationships? Or more importantly, is such an arrangement even healthy for the pastor, given the relational needs of clergy? Is there a way for pastors to hold healthy friendships in the church while also maintaining

---

Stott notes that *koinonia* has its roots in the word *koinos,* "common," and that *koinonikos* is the Greek word for "generous." *Koinonia* denotes a community of generosity, and in the case of Acts 2:42-44 (the first use of *koinonia* in the New Testament), we learn the early Christ-followers practiced *koinonia* as they "had everything in common" and "sold property and possessions to give to anyone who had need." As Stott notes, "these are disturbing verses. Do they mean that every Spirit-filled believer and community will follow their example literally?" Stott's observations underscore the high intensity of fellowship that may be involved in the life of Christian community.

their role as pastor, prophet, and priest to those whom they call "friends?" Or is the warning of prohibition ultimately the wisest word?

These are just some of the questions this study aims to address. The goal of this study is to describe what congregational friendships look like and how they function differently for the pastor than other friendships he or she may have. What does the discerning pastor need to know about this special relationship? What are the limits, and what are the potential consequences if these limits are unobserved?

The Research: Pastors' Practical Perspectives

To assist us in exploring the realities of friendship in pastoral life, we turn to wisdom and experiences of pastors currently navigating the intersection of personal relationship and pastoral leadership in the church. In this and the following chapters, pastors "in the trenches" of congregational life share their front line insights on the practical realities of friendship and pastoral life. I have chosen the scope of the research in this project to be qualitative in nature. As stated in previous chapters, the experience of friendship is a subjective one, making a qualitative look at the subjective experiences of pastors the most helpful way to uncover themes that reflect the experiential reality for pastors, at least at this time and place in our culture.

Behind this approach is a belief that there are few, if any, definite "shoulds" and "should-nots" that govern pastoral friendships other than the common moral and ethical guidelines that govern all pastoral relationships. As tempting as it might be to seek out a few objective measurements to speak definitively about whether or not a pastor can be friends with parishioners, or exactly how many friends a pastor should have to ward off isolation or burnout, such pronouncements may ultimately not be so helpful. Objective measures may be able to inform us with an interesting set of quantities, such as how many pastors have enough friends, how many friends the average pastor has, or whether or not pastors have as many friends as the general population, but none of these objective measures helps the pastor navigate the practical complexities of congregational friendships.

Furthermore, given the diversity in today's clergy, with the many personality styles, ministry settings, and denominational cultures, the qualitative approach simply makes sense. One could take as an example the diversity in personality and style the pastors in this project represented. Some considered themselves very private and slow to open themselves up to others. Others were self-declared as passionate extroverts, fueled by human interactions of all kinds. The latter would starve without numerous complex and interpersonal relationships, while the former would simply find that exhausting. The reader is invited, within the context of his or her own personality and ministry setting to respond with a "yes" or a "no" to the insights of the participants. Qualitative research allows for a sampling of voices to be heard, all the while giving the reader the privilege of gleaning from those insights what is practical and relevant to his or her ministry practice while leaving behind those that are not.

Thus, there is no agenda here to change any pastor's baseline opinions or beliefs about the nature of pastoral friendships. Instead, it is my hope that by giving exposure to the particular voices of these contemporary pastors on the issue, clergy can become more informed about the benefits, limitations, hazards, and particularities of a pastor's friendships. Therefore, to continue using the example of varying personality types, the guarded, private pastor ought to find in these pages insights and intentionality about the way they engage people they call friends. Likewise, the outgoing, friendly-by-nature pastor who has "never met a stranger" will hopefully become consciously aware of the many unconscious checks and balances that they employ in living such an open life before their congregants. Intentionality and insight are the goals. If pastors develop a deeper understanding of why they feel what they feel about pastoral friendships and move their reactions and responses out of the unconscious realm and into the conscious realm, then this project will have been successful.

About the participants, this research project represents a sampling of both male and female pastors in both mainline and evangelical congregations. All are active pastors ranging from ten to 29 years of congregational ministry experience. They averaged 19 years in congregational ministry. The group ranged in age from early thirties to mid-sixties. Eight were male. Two were female.[14] Seven described themselves as "evangelical" pastors while three claimed a "mainline" pastoral identity. Most of the pastors in the survey have led or are

---

[14] Given that the Barna Group reports that one in ten churches in the U.S. have female clergy, it was important to seek out female clergy for their insights into this subject. And while the ratio of women chosen for this study corresponds to the percentage of practicing female clergy today, it is admitted that the limited number of female clergy in this project represents a shortcoming of this study. Much has been written about the difference experiences men and women have with friendship, and certainly those differences would influence how female clergy experience friendship in the church. Certainly, female clergy may find the themes here skewed towards the male clergy experience. No pretense is made here that the female perspective has been adequately represented. Given the differences between men and women in the experience of friendship along with the unique challenges of female clergy pioneering their way through institutions with predominantly male leadership, further study of the female clergy experience friendships in the church in ways different than men would offer a significant contribution to the work of female ministers.

currently leading congregations in the central Pennsylvania region. Three in the study are currently pastoring churches in the Carolinas and Maryland. Only half were born and reared in Pennsylvania. Six of the ten have pastored in more than one region of the U.S. and were able to speak to the transitory nature of pastoral life and its impact on friendship formation. To protect the identity of the interviewees so that they could feel confident in being as open as possible, their names have been changed throughout the course of this paper.

The interviews were conducted with an established set of questions, presented to all participants. The questions were designed to be open ended. Much latitude was given to allow the participants to express how they felt and to go in whichever direction they felt important. Careful attention was paid to these "rabbit trails," for the assumption at the base of these interviews was that these pastors would take the research wherever it needed to go. If a pattern of comments emerged from outside the formalized questions, then these findings were considered significant. Follow up questions were aimed at following through with the thought of the interviewee, as careful attention was paid not to use follow up questions to direct or redirect participants towards a particular topic.

Names of the participants have been changed for the sake of privacy. Where particularities of the stories and insights that were shared would risk possibly revealing the identity of the pastors, these have been generalized. Where identifiable particularities have been used, permission of the interviewee was secured.

THEMES: Friendships Inside the Church

Throughout the course of the interview process, my goal was to identify themes and commonalities that emerged from the conversations. Therefore, what follows are the themes that emerged from these interviews. During the course of these conversations, as particular ideas and observations continued to recur and be validated by multiple pastors, I sought to link these observations together. While themes themselves do not represent "final conclusions" on the matter, they do, however, allow the reader to consider whether or not these themes connect with his or her experience as pastor.

While my quest to identify common themes was central to the interviews, I sought not to overlook individual insights unique to a single interviewee. In almost every interview, each pastor offered a unique insight unnamed by the others. In my reflection on these insights, I began to observe that these insights were singular not because they are not experienced by other pastors, but simply because that particular pastor's unique experience helped bring an embedded insight into the light of their reality. Many times, pastors shared unique observations that I had not before considered but yet were true to my own experiences and in line with the expressed insights and experiences of the other pastors. Thus, where these insights advanced the understanding of pastoral friendships, they have been included.

It is important to add that I, as the interviewer, do not claim to have a fully objective interpretation of the particular themes that emerged. My own experiences with friendship, my own experiences with congregational complexities, and my own feelings about the importance of friendships remained acknowledged throughout the course of these interviews and in the interpretation of the data. While I sought to give the voice of the interviewees ultimate preeminence in this study, I cannot claim to be outside this process. In this case, I, as the researcher, am a factor in this study and the interpretation of this data. Therefore, another researcher listening to these same interviews may describe the themes somewhat differently. However, it was my strong desire and hope to allow the common themes to emerge in spite of the reality of my own prejudices and experiences.

With this said, the following themes were interpreted as significant outcomes of the ten interviews that were conducted.

THEME: It is acceptable for pastors to have friendships inside the church.

One primary assumption I sought to examine in this study was the notion that at least a few pastors would offer an expressed prohibition against having friendships inside the church. However, one significant finding is that there was no suggestion at all among the pastors in this study that congregation members are "off limits" to pastoral friendships. In fact, it was commonly stated that congregational friendships are "essential," even "ideal." One pastor remarked, "This is the church. If you can't have friends in the church, where can you have friends?"[15] Given the value that these pastors place on Christian friendships, many consider the church the most natural setting for these relationships to form, despite the complexities introduced with the pastoral role.

Several described hearing the prohibition during seminary or from mentors in ministry. "'Set apart' by their ordination, they've been schooled to believe they can't have friendships with their parishioners."[16] While this prohibition may still be advanced in the exposition of ministry theory, actual practice seems quite different. The Theological Colloquium on Excellence in Ministry at Duke Divinity School, made up of pastors,

---

[15] "Dan," Interview with author, November 18, 2013.
[16] Bob Wells, "Friendship: It's Okay to Go There," *Divinity* 2, no. 2 (Winter 2003): 4.

scholars, and laity, contend that "not only is it okay for pastors to have friendships with their parishioners and with other clergy, it is absolutely essential," for, they add, "friendships lie at the heart of excellent ministry."[17] The colloquium members suggest that friendship tends to the "loneliness and isolation that plague so many clergy today."[18]

The pastors in this study affirmed the importance of having friendships within the congregation. While they admit to particular limitations with congregational friendships, most of the pastors struggled to imagine surviving the pastorate without having people they call "close friends" inside the church. The nature of these close friendships varied. Some were close friends with the elders and other leaders in the church. Others expressed that their closest friends were people who had little to no connection with leadership in the church, but were active in the congregation. Some described having "many friends" and some described "just a few."

Additionally, there seemed to be no theological concern on the part of these pastors about the exclusive nature of friendships. Rick, an evangelical pastor with 25 years of ministry experience, stated that having a close friend inside the church does not necessarily exclude others.[19] He, as a pastor and a Christian, continues to have a relational obligation to everyone inside and outside his church. Arguing against Kierkegaard's warning that friendship might be "too exclusive" for true *agape* love to abound within the Christian community, Rick offered, "*Agape* is about how I treat others. Friendship is what I choose to reveal about myself."[20] Agape, he said, calls the Christian to be faithful to the needs of others without condition, equal to others despite position, rank, or preference. But friendship offers a space for people to invest themselves into the lives of a limited few, based on an openness and honesty that, by its very nature, not everyone can receive. If *agape* means we relate to everyone the same way we relate to a friend, then the task is impossible. "We can't reveal ourselves to everybody," Rick said. "We're not wired for that."[21]

While it was acceptable and preferred for the pastor to have close friends in the church, the pastors often acknowledged the sensitivity being closer in relationship to a few congregants than with others. The pastors who spoke to this reality expressed little difficulty among their parishioners, offering that this is an expected reality among members of their church. Tyler, another evangelical pastor, stated, "There are different degrees of intimacy in the church. And 80 percent of the people

---

17 Wells, "Friendship: It's Okay to Go There," 4.
18 Wells, "Friendship: It's Okay to Go There," 5.
19 "Rick." Interview with author. October 11, 2013.
20 "Rick." Interview with author. October 11, 2013.
21 "Rick." Interview with author. October 11, 2013.

are in a group of 'I know your name,' and in the next 20 percent, there's the people you know much better, and the numbers die down until maybe one percent, you might end up having a true friendship with."[22] These varied levels of intimacy are an understood reality of church community, he said. Therefore, congregants expect that the pastor too will relate to the overall congregation on many different relational levels, with some as close friends.

Brian, another pastor in our study, shared that "if you have close friends in the church, you have to be careful that you are opening yourself up to everyone as their pastor, or at least be perceived that way, or people will resent the friendships you have."[23] He shared this story as an example:

> I was confronted at a church dinner one time by a man who enjoyed finding things I wasn't doing right. He was pretty angry. "Why don't you ever sit at my table? You're always sitting with the same people. It's like we're not good enough for you." I walked away feeling victimized and thought, "Why would I *want* to sit at your table if this is how you are going to treat me!" But I got to thinking about it later, and he was right. I was choosing where I sat based on my need to be with friends rather than my responsibility to be everyone's pastor.[24]

Brian learned that as long as he is perceived to be extending the pastoral relationship openly and fairly to everyone in the congregation, "they better accepted that I might have a closer relationship with a few people in the church."[25] This may explain why many of the friendships acknowledged by the pastors in this study were indeed quite private in nature and rarely on public display.

The reality, then, for the pastors in this study is that friendships will form. The question is how to have healthy friendships inside the church with the proper boundaries and discretion these friendships require? The concern of these pastors was not *whether* they could be friends with people in the church, but *how* they could be friends with people in the church. They wondered how the pastor can know who his true friends are, when he forms so many close relationships. How can the pastor have the kind of authenticity a friendship requires without violating her role as pastor? In the end, prohibition seemed unrealistic for these pastors. In fact, though they acknowledged that their role may limit how far into

---

[22] "Tyler," Interview with author, November 20, 2013.
[23] "Brian," Interview with author, September 29, 2013.
[24] "Brian," Interview with author, September 29, 2013.
[25] "Brian," Interview with author, September 29, 2013.

"friendship" they can go with some parishioners, a few expressed that avoiding friendships with congregants is to violate their calling to model Christian community and relationship to their congregation.

THEME: Trust and loyalty are most essential to close congregational friendships.

In the previous chapter, we observed that friendship is often difficult to define. Rather, it is better described as certain meaningful characteristics of the relationship are named. In the literature at large, a variety of descriptors emerged, connecting friendships with things like common interest, respect, and mutual affection, or in the case of more utilitarian friendships, mutuality, helpfulness, and shared life goals. Each respondent in this study was given an opportunity to answer the essential question, "How would you define a friend?" It was expected that a wide variety of responses would be given to the question.

Instead, respondents were almost unanimous in their response: "A friend is someone you can trust."[26] "A friend is someone who is loyal to the end, even despite your failures."[27] "I have to trust that I can say something to a friend and I won't have it come back on me."[28] Given the sensitive environment of the pastorate and the expectations placed on pastors, "trust" and "loyalty" were the descriptors most often named.

If a foundation of trust is built with a friend, then these pastors felt better able to enter into vulnerability in a way that they felt was not often welcomed in pastoral life. "A true friend accepts you who you *really* are."[29] Another emphasized, "A friend helps me to be myself."[30] In practical terms, one pastor said, "With a friend, I don't have to worry about what I say," for "a true friend accepts you no matter what they find out. And the more they find out, the more they accept you, and the deeper the friendship goes."[31] As one pastor said, "[A friend] loves you unconditionally through thick and thin."[32]

Trust plays an essential role in friendship. As once sociologist describes, "When we trust another individual, we are able to depend on and be sure of them in some way, having certain beliefs about how they will act/react."[33] These pastors place high value on the dependability and

---

[26] "Teresa," Interview with author, August 27, 2013.

[27] "Rick," Interview with author, October 11, 2013.

[28] "Laura," Interview with author, October 10, 2013.

[29] "Steve," Interview with author, September 9, 2013.

[30] "Brian," Interview with author, September 29, 2013.

[31] "Rick," Interview with author, October 11, 2013.

[32] "Dan," Interview with author, November 18, 2013.

[33] Mary Healy, "Civic Friendship," *Studies in Philosophy and Education* 30, no. 3 (May 1, 2011): 233.

predictability that emerges out of trust. "There has to be a level of understanding and trust," Teresa, a mainline pastor with the most number of years in ministry, offered. "A friend is someone I'd have to know would not violate my trust; that whatever I shared with that person would not get out to the congregation."[34] Steve, an evangelical pastor, described it this way:

> My closest friends are people who know who I am. I don't worry about what I say. I don't worry about telling them 'I don't really like them right now,' [*laughing*] or if they say something I don't like, because I don't feel that's something that will end our relationship. It will actually strengthen our relationship if we work through it.[35]

For many pastors, close friendships help to mitigate the stress associated with being "on guard" with the congregation. Teresa offered an anecdotal, if not archetypal story that demonstrates the constant internal dialogue that pastors have and the stress associated with it. She shared about her involvement with a church athletic group within her mainline congregation that often gathered at a local pub following a church athletic event:

> There I'm sitting with this dilemma. Do I have a beer with the rest of them, which I would *love*? But I'm here with a church group as a pastor. Should I do it? Should I not do it? It was just... The anxiety in me was just not worth it. So maybe my definition of a friend would be someone I could go out and have a beer with and that person be perfectly okay with it and not take it back to the church.[36]

Pastors accept that different standards are often applied to them than congregation members apply to themselves. The stress of being continually held to a higher standard is more tolerable when the pastor has a friend who will "let me be myself."[37] Laura, another mainline pastor, said, "I felt like in some ways [many parishioners] whittled away until they got what they wanted. But it was those people who I could really be me with who became really, really critical and important to me."[38] Therefore, with trusted friends, the pastor's role appears to be broad enough to encompass the more vulnerable aspects of their personhood. These

---

[34] "Teresa," Interview with author, August 27, 2013.
[35] "Steve," Interview with author, September 9, 2013.
[36] "Teresa," Interview with author, August 27, 2013.
[37] "Eddie," Interview with author, October 16, 2013.
[38] "Laura," Interview with author, October 10, 2013.

friends respect the pastor's role while allowing for the pastor to engage with deeper levels of vulnerability.

Ray Pahl describes trust as part of the "emerging modern ideal of friendship." Friendships, in achieving deeper levels of intimacy, base themselves not upon the "rules, regulations, or any part of the institutional order." Instead, "individuals, out of their own volition, work out how they should behave with their friends."[39] Friendship, then, achieves its intimacy based on rules unconsciously negotiated between friends themselves, rules that transcend the public expectations that institutions—and in this case, the church—have for their members.

This offers insight as to why the trust of a friend is so important to pastors. The "rules of the institution" place high, and often unrealistic, expectations upon pastors. The pastor is judged by how well he or she is following these unwritten, subjective, and often unattainable expectations that differ from congregation to congregation, and even person to person. How refreshing, then, is a pastor's true friend, who recognizes the impossibility of the pastor meeting these expectations in full. How significant is the close friend who negotiates a "new set of rules" that are outside the complex, institutional expectations of the pastor and tailors those new expectations to the pastor's own vulnerabilities, personality quirks, strengths, weaknesses, and unique qualities. The trusted friend knows that the pastor "being who he really is" may at times stands in conflict with the institutional expectations of that pastor. The trusted friend is there to offer grace and acceptance and provide sanctuary to the pastor's true self.

The pastors in this study expressed that this sense of safety is itself a critical component in their ability to survive the stress of the many expectations placed upon them. One pastor expressed that a good friend allows him to be "unguarded," when his role requires that he "always be on guard" in how he expresses himself to others in the congregation.[40] Therefore, for many pastors, trust became the overarching descriptor that encapsulated all other characteristics of friend.

THEME: Pastors often distinguish "civic friendship" from close friendship.

At the heart of what troubles pastors most about their close friendships in the church is the difficulty of knowing when congregants are pursuing true friendship and when they are pursuing friendship for reasons of personal advantage. "Everyone wants to be the pastor's

---

[39] Ray Pahl, *On Friendship* (Malden, MA: Polity Press, 2000), 61.
[40] "Tyler," Interview with author, November 20, 2013.

friend," more than a few pastors stated. Laura spoke directly to this issue:

> There are people who want to be my friend because of my role.
> There are people who are attracted to the role and power. When I
> first moved into the parsonage, someone called me and said, 'I've
> always been the pastor's friend. I need to come up and have tea with
> you.' Friendship was motivated by: If I can make Laura my friend,
> then she won't change anything in church.[41]

Most pastors were able to identify a number of relationships that appeared to have the quality of friendship but were colored by church politics or other less obvious factors.

While these types of relationships may sometimes be perceived as disingenuous or underhanded, they are actually an essential part of the functioning of an institutional system.[42] Institutions function through a network of civic friendships. They are "civic," in that the group functions with concerns for how best the organization can function for the benefit of the group and its constituents. But these relationships are also "friendly," in that they are rooted in very personal connections that aid in the process of reaching these larger goals.[43] They are described as "advantage friendships" in that these relationships provide an advantage to the members of the institution and the institution itself.[44] Yet in civic friendship, the friendship is secondary to the civic goals the individuals aim to achieve. As William Rawlings states it,

> [P]olitical friends devote themselves to pursuing a *common good.*
> They do things together primarily to serve purposes that transcend
> the specific desires of the individuals or subgroups performing the
> actions. Acting as political friends, they orient toward something
> more encompassing than their individual selves – a commonly
> recognized good.[45]

The friendships that form out of civic friendships are more than simply a resulting side effect of civic advancement. It is "advantageous to be interested in the character of fellow citizens with whom one comes in contact,"[46] for in the end, individuals are tending to the welfare of one another by first tending to the welfare of the organization. The aim of

---

[41] "Laura," Interview with author, October 10, 2013.

[42] Healy, "Civic Friendship," 229.

[43] Healy, "Civic Friendship," 231.

[44] Healy, "Civic Friendship," 231.

[45] William K Rawlins, *The Compass of Friendship: Narratives, Identities, and Dialogues* (Los Angeles: Sage Publications, 2009), 6.

[46] Healy, "Civic Friendship," 231.

civic advancement is the aiding of the individuals with whom the participants have relationship. While the ultimate benefit comes to the individuals involved, the ultimate priority is the advancement of the institution. Harkening back to what Aristotle spoke of as "friendships of utility," these kinds of relationships are essential to the advancement of society towards a common good.[47]

In church life, however, these designations are rarely clear. As identified earlier, the church is by nature a very personal community, meaning that the enmeshed blending of personal and civic relationships can be such that professional or institutional relationships can seem deeply personal. Congregants themselves may have little insight or understanding of any distinction between their civic loyalty to the good of the church and their interpersonal connections to those within the institution.

When a pastor enters this environment unaware, there can be a lack of clarity about the goal of the civic relationship itself, increasing the potential for personal woundedness. Pastors and congregants may perceive that they are in close relationship for the sake of the relationship itself only to discover in a time of institutional crisis that the institutional goals were held in a higher priority than the relationship itself. When this reality is understood in advance, pastors are often less surprised by something that may feel like "betrayal" or "disloyalty."

Throughout the conversations with our seasoned pastors, it became clear that pastors who held healthy close, personal friendships in the church were aware over time of the distinction between civic friendships designed to meet institutional goals and interpersonal friendships designed for its own end. While the term "civic friendship" was never used by any of the pastors in this study, the pastors were able to name it in other terms, such as by differentiating "acquaintances" from "close friends" or "friendships" from "professional relationships." Others simply named this by stating, "There are people who want to be my friend because I'm the pastor."[48]

As Laura offered, "We tend to see ourselves as teachers, preachers, caregivers, spiritual directors, or servants, but I've come to realize there are some who mainly see me in terms of my power in the church."[49] Pastors certainly find that the many power brokers in their congregations understand and respect the inherent qualities of these civic relationships. But it is not uncommon for the power relationship to position itself

---

[47] John M Cooper, *Reason and Emotion: Essays on Ancient Moral Psychology and Ethical Theory* (Princeton, NJ: Princeton University Press, 1999), 333.

[48] "Tyler," Interview with author, November 20, 2013.

[49] "Laura," Interview with author, October 10, 2013.

carefully in the background of what appears at first to be a genuinely personal relationship, as people in power relationships may not be openly aware of the political forces driving the relationship.

This relational complexity was often expressed negatively as a source of hurt and pain by many in the study. Many expressed a sense of suspicion around those who quickly or unnaturally sought out their friendship, for fear of the hidden motivations behind it. Laura offered a stark example of how these political forces can wound a pastor when the underlying motivations come to light:

> There was one person who desperately wanted to be my friend. He wanted to lend me his condo so I could go down and stay at the beach. All the past pastors had done that. Later, we were talking about adding deacons to the church, and I invited someone to come and talk about the way they use deacons at another church, and she was a woman. The next time I saw him, he called me a "bitch." How dare I bring another woman in to share my point of view? I just needed to do what he said I should do…. For me, that was my awakening.[50]

For Laura, this startling experience alerted her to the reality that a church member's desire to be in a close relationship with her may be shaped by other factors.

Several pastors suggested that the confusion between political relationships and personal friendships was heightened in the early days of their ministry, when they had little experience of these realities. Brian, who has twenty years of experience pastoring evangelical congregations, shared that he was "friends with everyone" when he first became a pastor. "Being 'authentic' and 'genuine' before your congregation was all the rage in those days, and I wanted the power distance between me and the people to be very low. So, it seemed like I had a lot of friends."[51]

Brian then enforced his first disciplinary action on a staff member who had demonstrated a continual pattern of deceptive behavior that failed to improve with corrective action. Working with the church's leadership, they made a decision to terminate the associate pastor's employment:

> We crossed every 'T' and dotted every 'I.' I mean, we went the extra mile to offer the pastor every opportunity to fix the situation. We went through all the proper procedures. We documented every step. We were very open with the congregation about the process. I

---

[50] "Laura," Interview with author, October 10, 2013.
[51] "Brian," Interview with author, September 29, 2013.

thought at that point things would come out okay. But I was so naïve. We had major fallout. People were angry. Some people left. But what hurt me the most were the people who I thought were my close friends who started to distance themselves from me. I was shocked. Those relationships were never the same. And that probably hurt the most.[52]

Brian expressed that he expected his friends to accept and support him in the face of these kinds of troubles. What he came to understand was that "their first loyalty was to the church. Their friendship with me was a means to another end." In his next congregation, he was better able to discern between "close friends and people I had close, friendly, pastoral relationships with," adding, "I don't get deceived quite as easily anymore."[53]

Tyler, another evangelical pastor with nearly twenty years of ministry experience shared of the pain associated with leaving a church after a brief season of conflict. Many of the friends he thought he had made along the journey were absent from his life in the years following his departure. When you open your heart to people and then that happens, it's hard. It's an unpleasant surprise. There are people who you thought were your friends, and then they're gone. And you wonder, was it "access to the throne? " Access to the pastor and the pulpit and the power? That disappointed me. That's why I find it really hard to be open to a certain extent[54].

Laura, Brian, and Tyler no doubt express the feelings of many pastors struggling in the aftermath of what felt like close personal friendships that were broken as a result of leadership decisions. The temptation for many pastors is to close themselves off from investing too deeply in people, especially those with power positions, who they consider acquaintances, professional relationships, or civic friends. While it may be simple enough to color those relationships as artificial, perhaps the more productive view is that they are simply a different kind of friendship altogether that can have great meaning when the goals of that relationship are properly understood. Brian added that after a few heartbreaking experiences, he was able to redirect his expectations:

I think those relationships work better now because I don't expect as much from them in terms of absolute loyalty. Those are for other friends. I have to be okay with the fact that I may make a decision about the direction of the church that someone I'm very close to may not agree with. And it may change our relationship. That doesn't mean it won't

---

[52] "Brian," Interview with author, September 29, 2013.
[53] "Brian," Interview with author, September 29, 2013.
[54] "Tyler," Interview with author, November 20, 2013.

hurt. It just means it's okay. And if I can't accept that, I'll probably fail to do what I'm called to do in the church out of fear of losing friends.[55]

Armed with that awareness, pastors can better engage civic friendships for what they are so that the pain is at least understood when political forces change the relationship. The pastor can then allow the relationship be what it is to the extent of what it can be.

THEME: The pastor's role often impedes the possibility of friendship in its fullest form.

As the previous theme begins to articulate, pastoral friendships inside the church are different. The pastor's position carries with it certain expectations and responsibilities that at times can conflict with the very goals of a close friendship. The pastor serves as leader, as spiritual guide, as prophet, as counselor. The pastor is a person of godly power and spiritual influence that congregants invite into their lives for the sake of their spiritual growth. Friendship, on the other hand, demands a mutuality that flattens any power advantage and places the friends on equal plane. Neither expects more of the other, and when friendships encounter a season of imbalance–where one friend does more "giving" than "receiving"–this becomes an acceptable variation, for the two friends expect that at some point in the future, the roles will be reversed and any "imbalance" will be restored.

This give and take inherent in friendships is not a natural characteristic of the pastor/parishioner relationship. The pastor is called to give, and the parishioner is invited to receive–whether it be guidance, challenge, insight, or direction. Whether or not it is fair or even biblically sound to make such associations, the reality is that pastors are seen in a different light than their parishioners. They are placed on the proverbial "pedestal"[56] and are expected to navigate the daily pressures of life differently than others, often with less angst, with more faith, and with only minimal (preferably humorous) failure. Limited self-disclosure is essential to the respect and admiration congregation members maintain for their pastor. Self-disclosure, when done inappropriately, erodes the pastor's sacred place in the parishioner's spiritual life.

It seems, then, that the high expectations parishioners have of their pastors is an opposing force to vulnerability and self-disclosure so essential to forming close friendships. Many acknowledged that the kind of church member who can tolerate this kind of vulnerability is rare.

---

[55] "Brian," Interview with author, September 29, 2013.

[56] Benjamin D. Schoun, "Can a Pastor Have Friends?" *Ministry: International Journal for Clergy* (July 1986): 9. Schoun defines the "pastoral pedestal" as "the projection of unrealistic qualities and exaggerated status upon the pastor."

These members possess a spiritual maturity and spiritual personality in which the pastor's vulnerabilities facilitate rather than restrict spiritual growth.

Steve offered such an example when speaking of the self-disclosure he could offer a close, childhood friend who later joined his church that he could not offer to the rest of his congregation. "I worked in two spheres. [With my childhood friend], I could really do and say things that a pastor wouldn't do and say with your congregants, or necessarily your friends in church."[57] Since his friend knew his personal history "from first grade on" and knew his life intimately "before I became a Christian and after I became a Christian," he could feel a greater sense of openness with his friend who recognized that "everything I do or say past or present is colored by my faith in Jesus."[58] Steve was able to provide spiritual leadership and guidance to his childhood friends without having to assume the traditional role. Instead, his authenticity as a person was an aid to their spiritual health. Steve, then, could be more vulnerable without risk of those words and actions being misunderstood.

This is likely an exception to the given realities of pastoral life. The reality is that for many in the church, the high levels of pastoral vulnerability required for intimate relationships to form come at a cost of pastoral vulnerability that some congregants are not ready to accept. The pastors in this study have a strong awareness of this, acknowledging that their role required a limited self-disclosure, even among people in the church they considered "close friends." Recognizing this reality, Rick remarked that when it comes to making friends, "I have to remember that it's not just about me. It's about them. [To be friends] they have to know things about their pastor, and be open to those things."[59] Some are not in a place of maturity to experience a pastor's vulnerability, he suggested. "They need me to be in a certain place for them to be comfortable," adding, "I'm afraid of violating that." For Rick, the line of appropriate self-disclosure is "always in the back of my mind."[60]

If the inherent dynamics of friendship, then, tend to stand in conflict with the inherent dynamics of the pastor/parishioner relationship, the question arises whether a pastor can ever really experience friendship in its fullest form inside the church. It appears that if a pastoral role remains fully intact, friendship pays the price. On the other hand, when friendship is formed between pastor and congregant, the pastoral role is then altered to make space for the friendship. One pastor questioned, "When a

---

57 "Steve," Interview with author, September 9, 2013.
58 "Steve," Interview with author, September 9, 2013.
59 "Rick," Interview with author, October 11, 2013.
60 "Rick," Interview with author, October 11, 2013.

church member becomes very close friends with the pastor, does the church member lose his pastor? Or when a close friend of the pastor decides to join the church, does the pastor lose his friend?"[61]

A finding that has emerged through this study is that the pastor's role inherently limits the possibility that the fullest form of friendships can be achieved between pastor and congregants. This is not to say that full and "complete" friendships do not take place between a pastor and a parishioner, but that it cannot occur without some lessening or redefinition of the pastoral role. Despite the difficulties of the pastoral role being redefined for the sake of friendship, it has not restricted these pastors from developing what they call "close friendships" in the church. In fact, nearly all were able to identify a few close friends inside the church. These pastors appeared to be able to operate with a self-regulatory restriction in their mind, knowing from person to person what each needed in terms of pastoral support and role. Some close friends required very little of the traditional "pastoral role" in their friendship with the pastor. Others required more.

This awareness brings a stress of its own. Rick shared about the thought process taking place in his mind when engaging in friendship activity with people he pastors:

> When do you stop being a pastor and when are you just a friend? When you're meeting with somebody, I constantly question, "When can I just play a game of something with you and when do I need to ask you a spiritual question?" Can I get together with somebody, play a game, laugh a little, and talk about sports and go home? The expectations are always going on in the back of my head. Do I need to do something spiritual here? Or if I *do* do something spiritual, am I going somewhere they didn't want to go, because they just wanted to play games and hang out? It's an occupational hazard. That wheel never stops turning in the back of my head.[62]

This continual monitoring speaks to the inherent cost to the pastor in maintaining close friendships in the church and why the argument is set forth here that many pastors may never experience the fullest potential of friendship with people inside the church. It appears that as long as those close friendships are formed inside the congregation, there will be an impact either on the pastor's role or on the friendship he or she is seeking to maintain.

Self-disclosure is not just an issue flowing from the pastor to the congregation. Relational self-disclosure often flows back the other way.

---

[61] "Eddie," Interview with author, October 16, 2013.
[62] "Rick." Interview with author. October 11, 2013.

Often congregational friends will feel a freedom to disclose things about themselves they would not normally disclose to their pastor. And in doing so, they feel they can tell things to the pastor that will also be safeguarded and held. This introduces another limiting factor that the pastor's role places on the full possibilities of genuine friendship. Often times, this is where the role of pastor conflicts with the nature of the friendship. James, an evangelical pastor with wide experience in pastoral leadership, illustrates this with a story:

> Whenever you're in a situation where you find out something you don't want to find out, you have to do something about it. In the context of relationship, I found out one of the elders was doing something he shouldn't be doing… [As pastor] I had to do something about it, and our friendship suffered. It ended, because I had to be the keeper of the ethic for elders rather than the friend who says, "Oh I understand. Don't worry about it."[63]

Citing another situation earlier in his ministry, James spoke of a fellow minister and friend in the congregation who began "confessing things to me I didn't know what to do with." The minister prefaced his comments with, "I'm just telling you this as a friend."[64] This placed James in a conflicting situation regarding what to do with that information. James felt compelled to act first and foremost on behalf of the church, leading ultimately to the dismissal of the minister. James shared that it is difficult for pastors to "compartmentalize" all that they hear when the roles of pastor and friend come into conflict.[65]

James changed the way he had heard self-disclosing information from friends in the church. "I've told people that, if you're about to tell me something as a friend, you have to understand that I'm your pastor. My position in the church trumps our friendship." Adding, "I feel a higher calling to that than I do being quiet about what you're about to tell me." James added that "this is only fair," noting that it's actually being faithful to the friendship by providing full disclosure about what it will mean for him to hear what his friend has to say.[66]

This challenge underscores one of the natural conflicts that exist between the pastor's roles as leader and as friend. As stated earlier, trust is an essential element in friendship, yet the pastor's commitment to the higher calling to the ecclesiastical mission often necessitates that he or she

---

[63] "James," Interview with Author, October 3, 2013.
[64] "James," Interview with Author, October 3, 2013.
[65] "James," Interview with Author, October 3, 2013.
[66] "James," Interview with Author, October 3, 2013.

cannot bear the secrets of friendship the way another friend might.[67] The nature of the pastor's role demands that the trust of the friendship rest secondary to the trust that the institution places in its pastor to advocate for the higher good.

In all of this, a few pastors were able to express that as long as they were functioning in the role of pastor, they would never fully be able to engage someone in their congregation as friend in the fullest and most complete ways possible. When asked about the possibility of true friendships with members of his church, Tyler offered,

> Yes, there are obviously friends [in the church], but is it to the level of the three that were with Jesus? Probably not while I'm their pastor. And I'm talking about a true, unguarded friendship, and I don't know about that. Will they love you no matter what? If you tell them you're struggling with some issue? I think that's why you have other friends. That might not be an area you can go to.[68]

Tyler added, "It's not that I'm not open and authentic with my church. I can reveal 95 percent of myself to the people I pastor. We're talking about that last five percent. And that's where intimacy is."[69]

This theme, therefore, carries with it both triumph and loss for pastors. The triumph comes in knowing that it is indeed possible to have very close relationships that pastors genuinely name "friendships", the very kind that can help to sustain the pastor through some very challenging and difficult times. But in the strictest terms, a pastor may rarely ever achieve the fullest potential of friendship with someone he or she pastors. That "last five percent" of a pastor's personhood may never be fully disclosed in a way that leads to the truest intimacy among friends. For the pastors in this study, this is a reality that "comes with the job" and one which most pastors accept as part of being an effective pastor with those they are called to serve.

The Pastorate and Contextualized Friendship

As we have seen through the course of these themes, pastor/parishioner friendships are different. When compared to the ideal of

---

[67] Ray Pahl, in *On Friendship*, 61. Pahl offers that "personal trust has a moral quality," and that true friends "should not betray each other." However, Pahl goes beyond this ideal to speak of the complexities involved when one friend places the other in a moral bind through disclosure of behaviors that "transcend the moral boundaries of their particular social worlds." It could be argued that a parishioner who discloses morally questionable behavior to a pastor is failing to be true to the friendship, given the bind that information places on the pastor.

[68] "Tyler," Interview with author, November 20, 2013.

[69] "Tyler," Interview with author, November 20, 2013.

friendship, pastoral/parishioner friendships can certainly feel limited, or even lacking. When we think of friendships, we imagine a relationship that is openly self-disclosing, mutual, straight-forward, rooted in common interests, secretive, and trustworthy. "Personal friendship... involves concern for the other person for his or her own sake" and "occurs for the most part in private settings out of public eyes and ears."[70] Therefore, the authenticity and quality of friendship appear significantly lessened when entangled with political or institutional forces, realities which often saturate the pastor's world. It is natural, then, for a pastor to wonder whether the friendships inside the church can be "true" friendships.

Consider, however, another angle. We must remember that the modern ideal of friendship is an ideal formed out of the context of modern life. It has not been the only context in which friendship has thrived. With one look at the long history of friendship, one sees that friendship has been defined and re-defined, shaped and reshaped, according to the many different contexts in which it has been placed. Aristotle defined the meaning of friendship in a world of political alliances among men. Early Christians defined friendship in a very communal sense, identifying *agape* as the higher ethic. During the Enlightenment period, friendship became more secularized and sentimentalized, as equality in relationships gained significance.[71] As we saw earlier, some feared the rise of capitalism would spell the end of friendship altogether, yet friendship overcame those gloomy predictions to survive in the form we know today. Friendship adapts to its context. Adams and Allan offer this:

> ...[I]ndividuals do not generate their relationships in a social or economic vacuum, any more than they do in a personal vacuum. Relationships have a broader basis than the dyad alone; they develop and endure within a wider complex of interacting influences which help to give each relationship its shape and structure. If we are to understand fully the nature of friendships, or for that matter of other personal ties, these relationships need to be interpreted from a perspective which recognizes the impact of this wider complex, rather than from one which treats the dyad in relative isolation.[72]

One could argue, then, that the sage warning that "pastors shouldn't be friends with their congregants" could be transformed into, "A pastor

---

[70] Rawlins, *The Compass of Friendship*, 5.

[71] See Brian Garrioch, "From Christian Friendship to Secular Sentimentality: Enlightment Re-evaluations" in Barbara Caine, ed., *Friendship: A History* (London: Equinox Publishing, 2009).

[72] Rebecca G Adams and Graham Allan, *Placing Friendship in Context* (Cambridge: Cambridge University Press, 1998), 2.

should be aware of the different shape of friendship in the church." The context of the church does not rule out friendship. It simply re-imagines it in a new context and a new way. If the pastor's friendships can be appreciated for the depths they are able to achieve in the midst of a challenging and complicated context, one may then see friendship as a highly functioning and highly valuable bond that is able to tend to the relational needs of the pastor.

What became evident in the interviews is that these accomplished pastors have found ways to have very meaningful friendships inside the church, even if the "ideals" of friendship as broadly defined are not always able to be achieved in each and every relationship. Pastors make it work. Pastors find a way to hold to their role and be open and vulnerable in friendship, and they accept and absorb the limits of each. When asked, "Do you have enough friends?" the response was surprising. Most have enough friends. Yet, more than a few expressed a longing for ideal friendships that are so difficult to find in the church. Yet, those who lacked a sufficient number of ideal friendships did not express a critical deficiency in their life of friendship. In other words, pastors may not have all the pieces of friendship in place in their lives, but many have what they need to make it work for them in a context that has natural limits placed upon it.

Dan expressed the both the limits and potential of friendship experiences he has known in the church. After expressing frustration about the limits of his friendship potential because of his position, Dan went on to tell about friends who journeyed with him on the challenging path of church planting. "I have true friends, those guys who have seen me at my worst, who've experienced those valleys in my life with me, have loved me through those valleys, have confronted me in those failures, and helped me walk through that and walked out back into the mountain tops with me."[73]

Despite the challenges of limited self-disclosure and the possibility that the ultimate ideals of friendship may not always be fully achieved, pastors manage to find a few who walk them "back into the mountain tops."

Jesus and "The Three"

As we ponder the intricate complexities of the pastor's congregational friendships, it may be helpful to know that contemporary pastors do not suffer these challenges alone. The gospels reveal that Jesus Christ experienced many of these same complexities during the course of his ministry. Jesus knew the task of being both friend and leader. Jesus

---

[73] "Dan," Interview with author, November 18, 2013.

knew what it meant to be misunderstood because of who he chose to be close to. Jesus knew the glares of critics who disparaged him as a "friend of sinners." Jesus knew the agonizing betrayal of a trusted associate, who only moments earlier had joined him at the table of sacred fellowship. Jesus knew the denial of one of his closest friends. Jesus knew what it meant to be let down by his closest three who failed to honor his moment of agony in the Garden of Gethsemane. Jesus knew what it was like to be abandoned at the moment of his greatest suffering, when he looking down from the cross only to witness the absence of many who were once his friends. Jesus also knew the comfort of seeing "the one whom Jesus loved" there at the cross, ready to assume care for Jesus' mother beyond his death.

Jesus entered the world in order to experience himself the very challenges of human creation and to absorb those experiences into the person of the triune God. Jesus too knows the experience of his followers who lead in an environment of continual pressure and expectation. Jesus knows the relational sacrifice that a spiritual leader makes in leading others.

Jesus also experienced the need, the joy, and the benefit of a "close few." Any guilt a pastor experiences in embracing some members more exclusively than others need only to observe Jesus' relationship with his twelve disciples. Jesus maintained his role as servant and leader to his twelve followers while entering more deeply into the lives of Peter, James, and John. While he related to each of his disciples in ways that were caring, confrontational, tender, and properly self-disclosing, he also related to Peter, James, and John in a distinctly more intimate way. John's gospel suggests that Jesus set himself even further apart with "the disciple whom Jesus loved."[74] Is Jesus violating his own commands to love one another? Is Jesus betraying the *agape* ethic by relating so exclusively with so few? Certainly not. Clearly, Jesus honored the experience of relating to those within his ministry on varying levels. Jesus related to many as "friend."[75] Yet, Jesus chooses to relate most intimately with a select few. The inference is clear: Jesus himself relates both to the broader world and to an intimate few in ways that are distinct and yet faithful to the *agape* ethic.

For Jesus, there was a personal price for leading the disciples and crowds who followed him. So too, pastors who surrender to the call may sacrifice being fully known by those who surround them week in and week out. They surrender to the realities of being misunderstood, being held to unrealistic standards, or being let down by those they thought

---

[74] John 20:2 (see also Matthew 17:1; 26:37; John 13:23; 19:26).
[75] John 15:15.

were close friends. Pastors may find the Paul and Barnabas story matches too often their own. But there is the hope that each pastor may find a David and Jonathan story, wherein loyalty and devotion outweigh position and agenda, easing the loneliness of the pastor's journey.

CHAPTER IV

Friendships Outside the Church

Where you go I will go,
and where you stay I will stay.
Your people will be my people and your God my God.
Where you die I will die,
and there I will be buried.
May the Lord deal with me, be it ever so severely,
if anything but death separates you and me.
—Ruth 1:16-17

This tender and heartfelt pledge from Ruth to Naomi has long stood among people of faith as a benchmark of ideal friendship. Ruth's life-long devotion would sustain Naomi through periods of bitterness and grief and ultimately lead to the extension of a family line destined to deliver the great King David and the coming Messiah. The friendship is an unusual pairing, of mother-in-law to deceased son's wife, of Israelite to Moabite, of old to young, of monotheist to polytheist. Whereas racial, familial, and religious differences have historically precluded the possibility of deep human connection, these two found that their human bond could transcend these social disparities. Ruth willingly surrendered the social stability of her religious heritage and familiar homeland for the hope of something more. In friendship, Ruth and Naomi achieved together what they could not achieve alone. Ruth's beauty and youth alongside Naomi's social and cultural connections enabled both to find footing again, leading to rediscovered significance in their lives.

The achievement of this non-traditional relationship points to meaningful possibilities for the pastor. Much like Naomi, pastors carry weighty burdens of past hurts and present-day challenges. Their job is like no other, requiring the pastor's close friend to accept certain peculiarities of this relationship. Given the great emotional energy pastors pour into in healing relationships within their congregations, the pastor may enter a close friendship as the needier friend. It may be that those who enter into close friendships with a pastor are initially, like Ruth, making the bigger sacrifice. Pastors may have little time or reserve to return the relationship to a complete state of balance. Pastors need much from their close friends: their time, their loyalty, their understanding, their listening ear.

Naomi and Ruth remind us that such a healing relationship is possible. Their story reminds us that close friendship can sustain us through disappointment and loss and reveal in us potential that might have been lost in the fray of stress and busyness. It opens up new possibilities for the pastor and reminds us that friendships can help one achieve what could not have been achieved otherwise. It reminds us that God has gifted us with this special relationship for the sake of our relational nourishment. But more than that, it reminds us that the close friend, the best friend, the intimate friend is simply a part of what makes life good.

The Importance of Non-congregational Friendships

Given the great gift that friendship is and the significance it plays in our lives, how does the pastor develop these very close friendships if, as we have seen, the congregational setting cannot always provide opportunity for the fullest ideals of friendship to flourish? As we have already observed, the natural limits of self-disclosure, pastoral role, and organizational politics chip away at the deep levels of intimacy and vulnerability the pastor hopes to achieve through friendship. The complexities of friendship in the congregation underscore the significance of the pastor's friendships outside this context. Friendships outside the congregation offer pastors relief from the continual pressures of the pastoral role, mounting expectations, and the need to "always be on." Since genuine friendship provides space for a pastor to "be who I really am," it becomes a place of respite that refuels depleted energy stores, reignites imagination, provides intellectual and professional stimulation, fosters a sense of togetherness, and combats feelings of isolation that may mount in the face of great stress. Friendship outside the church extends the hope of relationship without the stress of role expectation. They "strengthen the inner being and enable pastors to be more effective in the challenges of their work,"[1] while grounding them in a sense of normalcy that is often lost in the pastor's "glass house" world.

Yet despite the many healthy reasons for pastors to seek and maintain friendships outside the immediate congregational context, many pastors struggle to find and nurture such relationships. It may come as no

---

[1] Benjamin D. Schoun, "Can a Pastor Have Friends?," *Ministry: International Journal for Clergy* (July 1986): 9.

surprise that the pastors in our study had much less to say about friendships outside the church than they did friendships inside the church. Some could describe no close friend who is entirely set apart from the context of ministry. Those who did express having close and healthy friendships outside the church described troubling obstacles in maintaining those relationships. Pastors, in fact, described two significant limitations.

Limiting factor: Time

The significant time demands placed on the pastor for congregational ministry leave little time for most pastors to invest in the kind of quality, close friendships that relieve them of their demanding role. "Even if I had some close friends in the community," one pastor said, "I have no idea how I'd give it the kind of time it needs to be healthy."[2] Consider the scope of pastors nationwide. A 2001 Pulpit and Pew survey[3] of U.S. congregational pastors discovered that 72 percent do not take a regular day off. In their time commitment to the congregation, less than two hours of their work week is spent in community activities. Just under half said that having a private life apart from their ministerial role was "a problem." The same number said finding time for "recreation, relaxation, or personal reflection" was a problem, with an additional 18 percent describing it as a "great problem." Nearly half expressed difficulties in "having a private life" apart from their role as minister.

Michael, a pastor in our study, shared about a time he connected with a physician who had done research in an area of interest related to Michael's ministry. They were together at their daughters' preschool gathering when after a time of great conversation, the physician suggested they "get together sometime for a drink." Michael shared his immediate feelings. "Here he had put himself out there, and I'm thinking, 'I don't know when that's going to happen.'"[4] Michael reports never being able to follow up with that invitation to develop a closer relationship due to the overwhelming nature of his schedule.

Along these lines, the Pulpit & Pew study showed that more than a quarter of pastors felt that their work deprived them of adequate time with their children and spouses. If such a high number of pastors struggle to give adequate time to their own families, one can imagine how much less time is available to give to social relationships outside the scope of

---

[2] "Michael," Interview with author, November 4, 2013.

[3] "Pulpit and Pew National Survey of Pastoral Leaders" (Pulpit & Pew, 2001), accessed March 17, 2013, http://www.thearda.com/Archive/Files/Codebooks/CLERGY01_CB.asp.

[4] "Michael," Interview with author, November 4, 2013.

ministry. As Michael said in the telling of his story, "Between family and church, it's not easy to connect."[5]

Limiting factor: Opportunity

With limited time comes limited opportunity. Because the world of the pastor is often synonymous with the world of the church, many of the pastors described their social life as an extension of church life. Very few could describe activities that would situate them regularly outside the context of ministry and provide them opportunity to meet and develop friendships outside their immediate ministry context. A few named activities, like regular workouts at a local gym or participation in an athletic association, as a part of their routine beyond the walls of the church. Even then, most recreational activities that moved them outside the direct context of church life still often occurred with church friends or groups. With little time to spend outside of church and family, pastors had little opportunity to meet people unassociated with their ministry context.

Social Isolation and the Pastorate

These factors highlight a common problem among pastors leading to exhaustion and burnout, namely the problem of isolation and loneliness. Pulpit and Pew's 2001 national survey put numbers to the issue of isolation and loneliness. Just over half of pastors nationwide said that they occasionally feel "lonely and isolated in their work," with 17 percent expressing this in more serious terms.[6]

Bob Wells, in writing on pastors and their friendships, points to loneliness and isolation as "the single greatest predictor of overall job dissatisfaction."[7] Catholic priests who left the ministry within five years of ordination, he points out, named "isolation and lack of close friendships" as "one of the most important reasons [they] cited for quitting the ministry, second only to celibacy."[8] Wells points to the lack of healthy friendships as a factor. "The isolation this [lack of friendship] creates can ultimately lead to burnout. One can be constantly involved with people and yet be in need of friends."[9]

London and Wiseman, in *Pastors at Greater Risk*, lift up several factors that contribute to this loneliness. Pastors naturally face physical isolation,

---

[5] "Michael," Interview with author, November 4, 2013.

[6] "Pulpit and Pew National Survey of Pastoral Leaders."

[7] Wells, Bob, "Friendship: It's Okay to Go There." *Divinity* 2, no. 2 (Winter 2003): 5.

[8] Wells, "Friendship: It's Okay to Go There.," 5–6.

[9] Schoun, "Can a Pastor Have Friends?," 9.

as the pastor engages the work of sermon preparation, personal study and growth, and church administration, all of which push the pastor behind closed doors in "behind-the-scenes" work. Existential isolation occurs also, as the pastor continually accompanies people in crisis, after which the pastor is "left alone with his own questions about the ultimate issues of life and death." Geographic isolation, then, separates pastors from their extended families, collegiate and seminary colleagues, and childhood friends. Lastly, relational isolation as named in the previous chapter means that the pastor is "never allowed to be human – only 'pastor' or 'the Reverend.'"[10]

Wilson and Hoffman, in their book *Preventing Ministry Failure*, connect this isolation and loneliness to emotional burnout and ministry collapse.[11] They describe healthy intimacy not only as an antidote to loneliness, but as a "foundation stone of effective long-term ministry" for the pastor. Intimate relationships "are those in which others truly understand us, even if they don't agree with us."[12] Whether a friend, marital partner, or significant other, those with whom one has intimacy[13] "are familiar with our strengths, weaknesses and idiosyncrasies, and they still desire relationship with us."[14]

Furthermore, intimacy is a fundamental factor in shaping the pastor's personal worth and identity, or as Wilson and Hoffman describe it, the "who we are" as pastors. The intimate interactions one has with God, family, or friends, all contribute to the feelings one has about himself. But for Wilson and Hoffman, intimacy is only one of two fundamental factors that shapes a pastor's identity. The other is found in the pastor's sense of calling.[15] Because a pastor's calling is a "personal invitation from God" to serve in God's Kingdom work, a pastor gains a strong sense of who he or she is in the fulfillment of that calling.[16]

Therefore, it is of interest that Wilson and Hoffman connect intimacy and calling together in shaping the pastor's personal identity.

---

[10] H. B. London and Neil B. Wiseman, *Pastors at Greater Risk* (Ventura, CA: Gospel Light, 2003), 52.

[11] Michael Todd Wilson and Brad Hoffmann, *Preventing Ministry Failure* (Downers Grove, IL: InterVarsity Press, 2007), 40–41.

[12] Wilson and Hoffmann, *Preventing Ministry Failure*, 35.

[13] Wilson and Hoffmann, *Preventing Ministry Failure*, 34–35. Wilson and Hoffman address the reality that intimacy has become "a euphemism for sexual relations." Because "many in our society are uncomfortable speaking of sex directly, our culture has largely adopted *intimacy* as a substitute word, to the exclusion of intimacy's broader and richer meaning."

[14] Wilson and Hoffmann, *Preventing Ministry Failure*, 35.

[15] Wilson and Hoffmann, *Preventing Ministry Failure*, 27.

[16] Wilson and Hoffmann, *Preventing Ministry Failure*, 65.

For what logically follows is that success in one's calling is linked to the identity one develops through intimate, healthy relationships. If in the bruising and busy context of ministry, pastors fail to devote time and energy to healthy, intimate relationships, the pastor may then turn to more self-destructive, isolationist, and escapist behaviors. These range from obsessive behaviors (i.e. workaholism, overeating, excessive internet/TV use) to relational and sexual dysfunction (i.e. physical or emotional infidelity, use of pornography, sexually compulsive behaviors).[17]

Pastors are all too familiar with the outcomes of such behaviors, as the stories of ministry failure are not difficult to find. Once the pastor begins to fulfill these intimacy needs in dysfunctional ways and healthy intimacy begins to wither, the pastor's ministry is put at risk. Therefore, a socially isolated pastor has more to be concerned about than the weight of lonely feelings or the absence of good recreation. The socially isolated pastor is a pastor in jeopardy of falling into discouragement, feeling burned out, engaging in self-destructive behaviors, and ultimately losing his ministry.

THEMES: Friendships Outside the Church

Therefore, with this awareness, we turn to the matter of friendships outside the church. What follows is a picture of the opportunities and challenges of pastors today in real-world situations. What do those challenges look like? How do pastors work around them? How well do they relate to those outside the church? What are their resources for finding good friends away from their congregations? As we engage these questions, we once again will be introduced to themes as they emerged in the interview process. One note to consider is that for our purposes here, the term "friends outside the church" does not necessarily mean "secular" or "non-Christian" friends or even friends completely detached from the pastor's world of ministry. The reference is simply to the friends of the pastor outside his or her current and immediate congregation. Any relationships that pastors maintain in which their role as pastor is not a conflicting factor in their personal friendship is of interest to us as a "friendship outside the church."

THEME: Pastors find challenges in maintaining "close friendships" with ministerial colleagues.

At first glance, it appears that the most natural place for the pastor to find close friends may be with other pastors. Pastors share a bond of understanding that many outside the profession cannot provide. In fact, the 2001 Pulpit & Pew study discovered that nearly 90 percent of pastors

---

[17] Wilson and Hoffmann, *Preventing Ministry Failure*, 40.

expressed having satisfying relationships with fellow clergy. It appears also that friendships with colleagues are less impeded by the limitations of "time" and "opportunity." The congregation usually considers the pastor's interaction with other pastors, especially within his or her own denomination, as essential to the pastor's work; therefore, the pursuit of relationships with other pastors is one activity that can be pursued within the parameters of the pastor's busy work schedule. This means that in most pastoral settings, it may be less problematic for the pastor to make time to foster the relationship.[18]

Before pressing that point too far, however, it is clear that this relationship too has its limits. Busy pastors may connect on regular occasions through denominational meetings or ecumenical gatherings, but even with these appointed times, pastors often lack sufficient time to develop these relationships as deeply as they wish. Most of the pastors in our study described getting together on a monthly basis with other pastors. A few were able to develop weekly one-on-one gatherings with the pastors to whom they were closest. With all that pastors contend with in their schedules, and as valuable as collegial interaction is, this relationship too ultimately suffers from constraints of its own.

It is also clear that collegial friendships do not always provide the escape from pastoral role that the pastor hopes to find in his or her close friendships. The pastors in our study consistently stated that the central topic of conversation with other pastors was church life and church related issues. "They get it," one pastor said. "They know the stresses of ministry. They can bemoan with me a little bit. But that's just it. It feels like when I'm with them, ministry always comes up. And I don't necessarily want to talk about that all the time."[19] A few described the recognizable scenario of pastors comparing church size and success. When congregational concerns are embedded in collegial conversations,

---

[18] It should be noted that not all pastors have abundant access to ministerial colleagues. Pastor Brian described having a "host of pastor friends" when serving a large, suburban congregation, but when he relocated to a more rural pastoral context, "most of the pastors around me pastored small churches and worked jobs outside the church." When he moved into town, he wrote letters and emails to a dozen pastors in hopes of developing a few supportive relationships, knowing what his pastor friends meant to him in the previous church setting. "I got no response," he lamented. "It just wasn't a part of the culture of part time pastors to spend a lot of time with other pastors." ("Brian," Interview with author, September 29, 2013.)

[19] "Rick," Interview with author, October 11, 2013.

this colors the relationship in a way that hinders them from being the kind of close friendship the pastor is hoping for. While these conversations were certainly a place for our pastors to unload their stresses and to gain advice and commiseration, these relationships did not always lend themselves to the kind of deep personal bonds that are a healing characteristic of close friendships.

Added to this is the tendency of pastors to act as "problem solvers" to other pastors when the vulnerabilities of pastoral life arise in conversation. Rick said about pastoral friends, "Even though I feel I can tell them about my ups and downs in the church or even problems I'm having, I might hear, 'Oh, I know that too. How can I help you with that?' But sometimes, I just don't want to be fixed."[20] Rick offered the story of a time when he was facing a significant crisis in his church dealing with an extramarital relationship among two of his church leaders. Feeling wounded and overwhelmed by the situation, he sought the support of fellow pastors:

> The problem was that I reached out to some pastor friends at that time, and there were ones that just listened who were great, and there were other ones who tried to fix the problem. And I honestly, briefly despised them. "I don't need you to fix this. I'm not even asking you for advice. I just need you to be there right now because this is tearing my soul apart."[21]

Through that experience, he learned that even with colleagues, there are some who are "personal friends" and others who remain "professional acquaintances." For Rick, the difference was in the ability of his colleague to offer empathy and validation of feelings rather than advice and solutions.

Another complexity of collegial relationships mentioned by several pastors in our study is the use of the collegial relationship as an intentional "accountability" relationship. Eddie, a mainline pastor, described meeting regularly with fellow clergy with the specific intent of holding each other accountable to regular spiritual practices, sufficient time with family, and proper boundaries with staff and congregation members, to name a few. This became a "confessional" environment embedded in trust and confidentiality. This was a significant part of Eddie's development as a person and pastor, but he said these kinds of relationships did not branch out beyond this primary function. Therefore, while he described his fellow pastors as "good friends," he was unable to call them his closest friends. "When you're with your closest friends, you really don't get

---

[20] "Rick," Interview with author, October 11, 2013.
[21] "Rick," Interview with author, October 11, 2013.

together with a set agenda."[22] After reflecting on this, Eddie offered that the accountability group probably arose out of the fact that few of the pastors had close friends in their immediate geographical context with whom they could have an honest and confessional relationship in a natural way. "This group met that need that we weren't finding in other people in our lives."[23]

An interesting note in this study related to clergy friendships was how rarely our pastors ascribed "friendship" to their relationship with fellow staff ministers within their own congregation. While the topic of staff minister relationships may move us back for a moment into the subject of friendships *inside* the church, the complexities of staff relationships are an intricate reality for most clergy. The pastors in our study appear to have established clear relational boundaries with their fellow staff and expressed their relationship with staff in far more professional than personal terms. Few felt they could be friends with people they were supervising, since, as one pastor stated, "it was important that they see me as their boss."[24] Much like the other collegial relationships that have been identified thus far, relationships between ministers working together in the church are close and meaningful relationships, centered on common mission and working together "in the trenches." Many described a close professional bond, much shared humor, and many meaningful activities together, but few felt comfortable in describing them as close friends, at least while they were serving together in the same congregational context.

Developing these boundaries appears to be an insight that is discovered through time and experience. Brian describes a situation early in his ministry with a ministry colleague whom he supervised who he also considered a close friend. He describes the complexities of his situation when church discipline had to be introduced with this particular minister:

> My first instinct in the beginning was to reach out to him as my friend, but yet I was the pastor and came to realize that as much as I wanted to help him as a friend, I had to relate to him as the pastor of the church and his supervisor. I wish I had learned to maintain those boundaries early on, because I think it would have helped me deal with that situation much more effectively.[25]

As pastors develop the maturity gained through experience, as many of the pastors in our study have, the establishment of these professional

---

[22] "Eddie," Interview with author, October 16, 2013.
[23] "Eddie," Interview with author, October 16, 2013.
[24] "James," Interview with author, October 3, 2013.
[25] "Brian," Interview with author, September 29, 2013.

boundaries limits fellow staff from becoming close, personal friends in the deepest sense.

Despite these shortcomings to collegial friendship, however, most of the pastors were quite willing to call other pastors their "friends." Rick described several close and essential relationships with other pastors, but he identified them as being "in its own category of friend."[26] Collegial relationships offer key elements of friendship and are significant to the pastor's self-care strategy. Colleagues help to validate experiences, to remind pastors they are not alone, and to help them find fresh ways of navigating through the difficulties of church life. But our pastors did not always describe this important relationship in the say may they did their close friendships. The two relationships play essential but distinct roles in the pastor's self-care strategy.

THEME: Former congregants are a significant and meaningful source of close friendships.

One of the sobering challenges to forming close congregational friendships, as we observed previously, is the institutional concerns that infuse complexity into the pastor's personal relationships. Civic loyalties often compete with a congregant's loyalty to the pastor, leaving the pastor wondering if the friendship can survive conflicts and disagreements. This, along with the complexities of role expectation, lessens the possibility that close and nurturing friendship will be formed.

Our pastors report, however, that this complication greatly diminishes once the pastor leaves the church. Once established in a new congregation, pastors are free to form very close relationships with former congregants without conflicting agenda. Teresa reported, for instance, that one of her three closest friends was a former colleague and director of Christian education in her congregation. "It was not until I left [the church] that our friendship really took off."[27] James expressed this as well. "My associate pastor who was with me at [my church], we became friends after I left. We moved from being colleagues to friends.... Our relationship transformed."[28] Because he left to form a new congregation in the area, James was able to remain in close proximity to his former congregants. Without the pastoral responsibilities attached to those relationships, they began to take on new life, and close friendships were able to form out of those relationships.

James's story illustrates this theme most powerfully and reveals the potential significance of friendship with former congregants, for after

---

[26] "Rick," Interview with author, October 11, 2013.

[27] "Teresa," Interview with author, August 27, 2013.

[28] "James," Interview with Author, October 3, 2013.

leaving his first church to form a new church, James was invited ten years later to return to the planting church to take on a different pastoral role within the church's sizable pastoral staff. Once leaving the church plant to return to his former church, he was not only able to see new friendships form out of the church he planted, but James was returning to pastor people he had formed close friendships with after leaving the church the first time. "The people I grew close to when I left are still here. When I came back, we were able to maintain our friendship." But he adds, "Our friendships have been maintained, but they're just different."[29] James had to carefully re-introduce the boundaries he once knew with them so that loyalties to the church and his calling could find their proper place again. However, because of the long history James had with his close friends, both James and his friends were able to absorb the realities of his role into their relationship so that their good friendships could be maintained in a way that was healthy for James, his friends, and the church.

James's ability to maintain meaningful friendships in and out of these transitions and do so in a way that meets his friendship needs underscores the potential each pastor has in forming close friendships with former congregants. In both pastoral settings, James seized the opportunities to form close and meaningful friendships with former congregants and staff ministers. Though not all pastors will enjoy such a circumstance, James's story underscores the fruitful possibilities ahead for pastors who transition in their ministry within a relatively close geographical area. With time behind him, James was able to develop trust in friendship that many pastors struggle to find in ministry.

Alongside the story of James's success are the experiences of other pastors who were able to speak to the challenges involved in developing close friendships with former congregants. Brian described changes in his congregational relationships after he left his congregation to serve a position in another ministry in the same region as his former church. He describes this move as having a "sifting effect" on the close, pastoral relationships he had formed in the church:

> I was excited to see what would happen. I was close to a lot of people in my church who I could certainly describe as "friends." At first, everyone worked hard to get together to maintain our friendships, but after a few months, it started to become clear who would become real friends to me and who would be moving on.[30]

---

[29] "James," Interview with Author, October 3, 2013.
[30] "Brian," Interview with author, September 29, 2013.

Brian expressed some surprise at how it turned out. One couple he thought would be his closest friends "fell away pretty quickly." He imagined this might be a possibility. "They were on our worship team and we got together every week for practice and were really close. But we never did anything together outside the church." Brian surmised that because they had never developed a relationship outside the context of the tasks of church life, there was little to no routine to nurture their relationship outside that structure. "Without the worship team to get us together every week, [the friendship] just wasn't going to happen."[31]

Citing another friendship that did hold together after he left the congregation, he described having connections beyond the church while he was pastor:

> Another person who was also on the worship team ended up becoming our close friend after we left. But the difference was, she and her husband lived much closer to us, and we would see them quite a bit at our kids' sports activities since our kids played together. So we saw them pretty regularly after we left, which turned into having dinner together and having lots of conversations that weren't about the church. They are really good friends now.[32]

In addition to this "sifting effect," other pastors spoke to the challenge specifically involved in leaving a troubled ministry context. Eddie left a church under difficult circumstances and noted how close he had grown to those who had supported him through the difficulty. When he left the area, he maintained close contact with those he had grown close to, but found it difficult to transition the relationship outside the context of conflict. "When you've been in the trenches with people and then you leave, you still have a really close bond with them. But the difference is, the church drama is behind you now. The question is, can you learn to talk about something else?"[33] Eddie and others expressed this as being a challenge, reporting feeling particularly close to people they had "gone into battle with" in their last days at their church. But not all those pastors were able to transition those friendships outside of the church, since the tension that drew them together was no longer present. Eddie added,

> I can think of a couple I was really close to. They became really good friends because we dealt with so much church drama together. They supported me through some really hard times, so we had this

---

[31] "Brian," Interview with author, September 29, 2013.

[32] "Brian," Interview with author, September 29, 2013.

[33] "Eddie," Interview with author, October 16, 2013.

deep bond. But then when I left, and they would come to visit, all we could talk about was the church. We would relive the pain and hurt all the time. And after a while, the energy from that spent itself out, and the thing that helped our friendship form was gone. They still are our friends, but it's not the same.[34]

While the transition from parishioner to friend has its challenges, the reward of friendship that grows out of relationships with former congregants outweighs the difficulties. For the pastors in our study, former congregants provided the greatest source of close friendships and often the most meaningful.

Tyler describes forming "three close friendships" while he was in his previous church. One particularly close friendship was formed early on in his pastorate. "He was on the search committee when I came and was a big supporter of mine. We just became very good friend." Tyler felt close enough to him that he consulted with him when he was considering leaving the church. "There's only one or two you can do that with." They remain close friends today and maintain regular contact. "It was an intimate relationship, and things changed even more so for the better after we left." The relationship survived and grew because "it was more than a pastoral relationship. He's a true lifelong friend."[35]

For Tyler and others, great meaning is attached to relationships formed in the church that later transcend the congregational contexts and geographical moves. One struggle is that it may not always be evident while the pastor is currently serving the congregation who those friends will later be. For those pastors who left these congregations under some duress, these were described as "redemptive" in nature, for the close friendship that survived the transition was often the good that was salvaged from the troubled context of ministry. For others, these serve as the close friendships that will sustain them in a new ministry context where the pastoral role plays into the nature of the new relationships. The successful growth of a friendship after a particular congregational context gives hope that in the future, new friends will one day form out of the congregation the pastor currently serves. As one pastor said, "I have no idea who my true friends will be when I leave here one day, but I know that I'll have some, and that's something to look forward to."[36]

---

[34] "Eddie," Interview with author, October 16, 2013.
[35] "Tyler," Interview with author, November 20, 2013.
[36] "Dan," Interview with author, November 18, 2013.

THEME: Some of pastors' closest friends first know them outside their pastoral role.

In nearly all the interviews, pastors consistently shared their list of "best friends," even though this was not directly solicited. Of note was the fact that well over half of the interviewees named a "best friend" who knew them before they ever held the title of "pastor." For some, it was a childhood friend. For others, it was a college or a seminary friend. A few named someone they worked with prior to being called into ministry. Some named their youth group friends from their childhood congregation. Consistently, pastors named these as their most loyal and lifelong of friends. None expressed any role conflict and expressed that with these friends, their becoming pastors did little to lessen the character of their friendships.

Steve was arguably the most outgoing of all the pastors in this study and carried the widest network of friends. For Steve, his childhood friends were his most significant friendships. He regularly reached out to these friends despite being a significant geographical distance away. Interestingly, these were all friendships formed prior to his becoming a Christian, and certainly prior to his becoming pastor. Steve is a conservative, evangelical pastor and describes many of these childhood friends as non-believers. He says he is "diametrically opposed" to many of their points of view. But for Steve and his friends, these are not issues that divide them. "When we talk about things and we disagree, they know I love them. Because of all that time and because of all that life we have lived together and they know me and my heart, they know it's not something that will come between us."[37]

Steve contrasted this with meeting new people in the context of ministry. "Most people who just get to know each other and then suddenly realize these disagreements begin assuming a lot of things about the other person that may not be true. I don't get that with my friends."[38] He adds that "we've known each other for 30 years," suggesting that the time and shared experiences across lengthy sections of one's life holds the relationship together beyond differences. "I call it 'relationship capital.' When you build up all this capital, it's really difficult to squander it all away in any one given moment [of disagreement]."[39]

Due to the distance often involved in these relationships, pastors expressed that it is quite common for significant amounts of time to pass between contacts. One pastor said, "I'm not offended if I don't get a call for six months from one of my friends. We don't assume the worst about

---

[37] "Steve," Interview with author, September 9, 2013.
[38] "Steve," Interview with author, September 9, 2013.
[39] "Steve," Interview with author, September 9, 2013.

one another. We know we love each other and when we get together, we just enjoy the time."[40] Distance and time becomes acceptable components of the relationship. Eddie described having several friends from seminary who "I probably only talk to once a year, or even once every *few* years. But during the biggest struggles of my life, these are the guys I call, and we pick up right where we left off as if we've never been apart." He described these friends as "the ones who get me" and "will understand what I'm going through because they know me better than anyone else."[41]

Despite the length of time that can pass before these old friends reconnect, many pastors described intentionally seeking out these friendships to spend significant time with. Steve, for example, arranged to meet a childhood friend in another state to "hang out for a weekend."[42] James[43] and Rick[44] both vacation almost annually with friends from their past. In fact, those who mentioned spending a week or a weekend with old friends described feeling great freedom and acceptance from the people who knew them for who they are.

James, in fact, maintained such a close relationship with a college friend that the friend and his wife relocated from a neighboring state to live close to James. "They are like our family," James said.[45] As each one began losing their parents in death, the two couples found that they had a "family-like" relationship in one another. When James's friend's wife was diagnosed with a serious illness, the couple realized they were far away from family and support. "They've moved to be near us so they could have some close support. They came back and joined our church, and it's been amazing to have them in our lives like this."[46] James spoke about what it meant to have these close friends as a daily part of his life again. "It's just different. We haven't lived near each other in such a long time, we're still getting used to it. It's not quite normal yet. But our friendship is… well, it's great." With the distance from their own families, these friendships "are a bigger deal. The closer people to me in my life are my friends, not my family."[47]

Just as friends from the pastor's past can become like family, family can also become friends. Tyler named a brother-in-law as one of his

---

[40] "Steve," Interview with author, September 9, 2013.
[41] "Eddie," Interview with author, October 16, 2013.
[42] "Steve," Interview with author, September 9, 2013.
[43] "James," Interview with author, October 3, 2013.
[44] "Rick," Interview with author, October 11, 2013.
[45] "James," Interview with author, October 3, 2013.
[46] "James," Interview with author, October 3, 2013.
[47] "James," Interview with author, October 3, 2013.

closest friends. "He knows all my issues and there are no repercussions, and I don't have to worry about seeing him at church. He's not just my brother-in-law. He's my dear, dear friend."[48] In his brother-in-law, he has a recreational friend as well as someone he can speak to about issues that would be off limits to others in his life.

Tyler also illustrates the significance of losing a close friend of someone outside the church. Tyler was grieved to learn that closest friend died tragically. Tyler met him in the community outside his pastoral role and became very close friends with him. 'I could be who I was rather than 'Pastor Tyler.'"[49] He did later join Tyler's church and maintained a personal relationship with after he left his church. Tyler pointed to the fact that this friendship could transcend his ministry as what made it most meaningful. "When he died, I realized I lost a life-long friend. I thought we'd grow old together."[50] Tyler illustrates how valuable and seemingly irreplaceable these types of friendships are for many pastors. Because of the challenge of time and opportunity in forming friendships with people outside the church, when these relationships do form, they attain great value for the pastor. As Tyler said, "Now that he's gone, I'm not sure I'll ever have anything like that again."[51]

Whether it was a childhood friend, a community friend, or a "life-long" friend, nearly all of our pastors found that having friends outside the context of their immediate congregation had great meaning to them. Though few named these relationships as a direct "antidote" to burnout or stress, each one did describe themselves as being relaxed, unguarded, and true to themselves while engaged in these friendships. Robert Bell, in his book *Worlds of Friendship*, describes the significance of these kinds of friendships. "One result may be self-confirmation: [friends] gain a sense of who they are and something about their own self-worth. Or it may be a personal change in perception."[52] For the pastors in our study, these life-long friends who knew them beyond their title and accepted them for who they are seemed to provide them a personal sense of their own value and worth as a person.

Much has been written about the personal cost of ministry to the pastor. Pastors pour out themselves to those they serve, often to wonder about their own effectiveness and worth should their efforts be met with criticism or a sense that what they do is not enough. Friends who know

---

[48] "Tyler," Interview with author, November 20, 2013.
[49] "Tyler," Interview with author, November 20, 2013.
[50] "Tyler," Interview with author, November 20, 2013.
[51] "Tyler," Interview with author, November 20, 2013.
[52] Robert Bell, *Worlds of Friendship* (Beverly Hills, CA: Sage Publications, 1981), 14.

the pastor beyond their title and accept them outside of that role remind pastors that while they may be the target of much critique in their role, they are beloved outside their role. No matter what the pastor faces while "on the job," these few, but significant, friends sound another message–a message of unconditional acceptance and deepest validation of who the pastor is as a beloved human being.

Before transitioning away from the themes of this chapter, it is important to note two other observations that rise to our attention primarily for their absence in the interviews. First, none of the pastors in this study described their relationship with their spouse with friendship language. It was thought that in the struggle that pastors have in forming friendships that pastors might refer to their spouse as their "best friend." Perhaps, once again, the collective experience of the pastors in this survey accounts for why pastors shied away from placing those expectation onto their spouses. These pastors seemed to clearly understand that a close and supportive spouse does not, nor should they be expected to fill the space left in the absence of friendships.

Second, social media played only a supportive role in friendship and never appeared to be a substitute for face-to-face friendship. Given the rise of online social networks, pastors could easily begin to feel that they had the supportive friendships they need primarily because of a wide array of online connections with friends past and present. In fact, the pastors who did reference social media expressed that none of what they are looking for in friendship can be had purely through online interaction. They hungered for friendship that goes far beyond that. For those who interact regularly through social media (and those numbers were surprisingly fewer than expected), it was a way of staying connect until such a time as they could be face to face with their friends.

Friendship and Freedom

Deep and abiding friendship has freedom at its heart.[53] Friendship exists as a "freestanding bond"[54] in a freely formed relationship held together by freely chosen obligation.[55] Thus, it might be said that, for the pastor, the significance of friendships outside the church is its freedom. Under the spotlight of expectations and demands, it is not unreasonable for the pastor to crave the freedom to be unwatched, to be authentic, and to be free to be who she is. Friendship provides such a space.

---

[53] William K Rawlins, *The Compass of Friendship: Narratives, Identities, and Dialogues* (Los Angeles: Sage Publications, 2009), 1.

[54] Rawlins, *The Compass of Friendship*, ix.

[55] Rawlins, *The Compass of Friendship*, 9.

Yet, as we have seen, a pastor's friendships with his or her congregants are apt to be complicated by the very expectations and demands that often impede true friendship. Parishioners have a very reasonable expectation that the pastor will be there for them in ways that are self-sacrificial or even burdensome and will live up to a role that is significant to the congregant's spiritual development. The personal friendship between pastor and parishioner is secondary to the professional relationship between pastor and parishioner and the calling of the pastor to the greater needs of the church.

While close friendships with members inside the church bring satisfaction and nourishment in many circumstances, the pastor's friendships with people outside the immediate sphere of ministry is something altogether special. The close friend outside the parish context is an island of safety, freedom, and blessing for the pastor. In this safe place, the pastor finds a reprieve from the ongoing efforts to balance role and relationship. The pastors in our study described friendships outside the church in different terms. With these friends, the appropriateness of vulnerability was never in question. Guardedness was laid aside. Support was unconditional. Though time with these friends is often brief, it is a time of concentrated renewal. A few moments with a friend untangled from the pastor's congregational climate can infuse significant energy and stamina back into the pastor's being.

With the limits and possibilities now set before us for friendships both inside and outside the church, we continue to be faced with the reality that pastors not only have fewer close friends than they desire, but that the environment which prevents pastors from developing close friendships is not likely to change anytime soon. In presenting these themes, my hope has been that pastors will come to a greater understanding of the complex milieu in which they seek out close friendships. With greater understanding comes the possibility of heightened intentionality in fostering the close relationships the pastor does have. As we now turn to the final chapter, we enter in search of a few conclusions about the importance of close friendships to the pastor's wellbeing along with some fundamental guidelines about how pastors can go about finding and maintaining friendships in their ministry context.

CHAPTER V

Friendships and Today's Pastor

As soon as he had finished speaking to Saul, the soul of Jonathan
was knit to the soul of David, and Jonathan loved him as his own soul....
And Jonathan stripped himself of the robe that was on him and
gave it to David, and his armor, and even his sword
and his bow and his belt.
—I Samuel 18: 1,4 (ESV)

Friendship is as natural as the air we breathe. Or so we are told. It feels that friendship has such an organic splendor that friendships appear to form with great ease and unpremeditated effort. Furthermore, to analyze it is to contradict its nature and mar its beauty. Likely, most pastors practice friendship out of this exalted backdrop, leaving it a largely unexamined component of their relationships. Therefore, the dynamics of friendship unwittingly swirl about them, and unbeknownst to them, influence their relationships and ministry in ways of which there is no awareness. One wonders whether effective pastors can afford to engage such intimate relationships without an understanding of the impact of these relationships both on the pastor and the congregation. Even though pastors are provoked to think critically about so many facets of ministry, few pastors have been invited into the balcony of their relational life to observe the dynamics of their friendships.

In concluding this study, I offer such an invitation. I summons the pastor to the balcony of their relational life to hear the gentle detached voice of awareness illumining the amazing forces at work in our most cherished relationships. The intent of this project has been to present pastors with a much fuller picture of this seemingly organic relationship, for there is much to consider when the pastor chooses a friend or chooses to be a friend. Armed with awareness, pastors can incorporate healthy friendships into their lives in a way that aids their own self-care and relational effectiveness. Educated in the nature and impact of one's friendships, pastors are then able to marshal the critical support they need to function more effectively as relational beings.

As this study moves towards its conclusion, these last pages mark my effort to bring both motivation and practicality to the practice of pastoral friendships. My hope is to motivate pastors to act more intentionally in finding and sustaining friendships. Beyond the motivational is the practical. I hope to offer a few basic practices, or ways of thinking, that will lead to the development of more meaningful and fruitful friendships.

David, Jonathan, and Ideal Friendship

For pastors, motivation is often found first in the encouragement of scripture. In that spirit, I draw us back to the biblical text to one of the world's most inspirational friendships. The friendship of David and Jonathan[1] grants us a rare and meaningful look into what was a very personal and highly secretive relationship among two very powerful men. As Jonathan and David first meet, King Saul's suspicion of David is on the rise. Saul's mental and emotional stability is wavering while David's popularity is rising. Meanwhile, political forces are moving Jonathan ever closer to the throne, and yet the reader knows that divine forces have already been working against it. God has already placed His divine anointing upon David, who is destined to lead the people of Israel as their next king. The course is set towards irreversible conflict.

As the political pieces unfold prior to David and Jonathan's first meeting, one would naturally presume that only one possible "relationship" could exist between the two men: a violent and bloody one. The two seem to be on a collision course towards war for the throne. With this, the scene that unfolds in 1 Samuel 18 is a surprise to the reader's natural expectations. The text offers that upon their meeting, Jonathan becomes "one in spirit" with David.[2] The friendship that unfolds is of such force that the seemingly unbending political realities yield to a beautiful friendship. Jonathan, the text says, "took off the robe he was wearing and gave it to David, along with his tunic, and even his sword, his bow and his belt."[3] The act of surrendering his robe was a symbol to David that Jonathan was transferring his right to the throne.[4]

The connection between the two is of such force that Jonathan and David are often described as "soulmates."[5] Their relationship represents

---

[1] I Samuel 18-20.

[2] I Samuel 18:1.

[3] I Samuel 18:4.

[4] Walter Brueggemann, *First and Second Samuel* (Louisville, KY: John Knox Press, 2012), 136.

[5] Meir Shalev, *The First and Second Books of Samuel* (Edinburgh: Canongate Books, 1999), ii.

the deepest level of friendship one could hope to experience, with David and Jonathan laying aside all the contrary forces that could stand in the way of friendship. Jonathan sacrificed the interests of the family lineage for the sake of his allegiance to David. The relationship was one of enormous self-sacrifice and fierce loyalty.

What caused such a vibrant and instant connection? The text says that the souls of the two men were "knit" [6] together. But what was the acting agent instigated such a bond? Interestingly, regarding the knitting of their souls, the text leaves this in the passive voice, leaving the initiating force unnamed. This absence of a clear explanation has led many to fill the gap with their own ruminations. A growing minority of commentators view the relationship with a "homoerotic subtext," [7] suggesting that no other explanation could justify the deep connection. On the contrary, the mystery of the text is actually quite fitting to what we know of deep friendship. While certain elements like common interest and reciprocity help bring a friendship into being, the underlying reasons why some people connect as friends while others do not lies more in the realm of reverent mystery than the world of easy descriptions and precise measurements. With respect to this mystery, Walter Breuggemann identifies their bond as both an "emotional attraction and a political commitment." [8] It is evident that David and Jonathan experience the deeply interpersonal binds of friendship. Out of the intimacy of friendship comes action. The relationship plays out in an act of political loyalty, whereby Jonathan lays aside his own ambitions inherent in his right to the throne.

If there was ever an ideal friendship, perhaps this is the one. David and Jonathan relate intimately not for reasons of political advantage or civic cause or sexual fulfillment—reasons that explain the formation of many a relationship—but simply for the sake of itself. They relate together simply for the sake of one another. Perhaps this is why this particular biblical friendship holds our attention so well. In a world where contemporary relationships often function as "advantage friendships," subtly weighed down by personal interests, the need to get ahead, or the attainment of personal achievements, the modern aching for a true friend is significant.

Pastors may feel this more acutely, given how possible it is to feel "alone in a crowded room." Pastors are highly connected people, known for being fully saturated in a myriad of relationships. Yet many of these

---

[6] ESV, KVJ, NASB, and RSV translate the Hebrew verb as "knit." Others (NRSV) use "bound."

[7] For an example, see Bruce Gerig, "Jonathan and David: An Introduction," *The Epistle*, 2005, accessed January 17, 2014, http://epistle.us/hbarticles/jondave1.html.

[8] Brueggemann, *First and Second Samuel*, 136.

relationships are congregational or pastoral or collegial in their essence, meaning that they are relationships of expectation. These are relationships in which a role is being fulfilled. These relationships are why pastors enter ministry, for they are sources of the meaning and fulfillment that a pastor achieves in ministry. But are they always self-balancing? Do they refuel the pastor equal to the energy they require? Pastors inherently know that the joy of these relationships comes with a personal price, and that the effects of the relational deficit is tended to only through periods of retreat, recreation, spiritual nourishment, and relational intimacy. Without periods of restoration, burnout is an inevitable certainty. Thus, the need for a committed friend is strong.

The story of David and Jonathan, then, illustrates just how meaningful a close friendship could be for a pastor. Several observations are worth noting. First, Jonathan's loyalty to David was one in which political interests were surrendered for the sake of the friendship. The importance of this in regards to civic friendships and church politics has been expounded upon in the previous chapters and need not be repeated here. What is important to underscore here is how difficult it is for pastors to achieve the fullest forms of friendship with congregation members. Unless the congregant is able to consciously surrender his or her political and congregational interest in favor of personal loyalty to the pastor, it is difficult for the closest kind of friendship to form. It adds to the importance of the friend outside the context of the pastor's immediate congregation, for that friend has little political interest to complicate the relationship. Clearly, Jonathan's willingness to surrender his power at the forefront of his relationship with David is why the relationship could take on the ideals of friendship.

Second, Jonathan and David's friendship points out a nagging reality for pastors—one that may be difficult for a pastor to admit. Pastors need a friendship in which they can be needy. It is not beyond reason to note that Jonathan was the greater giver in the give-and-take of their friendship. In fact, one Jewish writer points out this imbalance by pointing to the language of love in First Samuel. He notes that the use of the verb "love" in the story of David and his relationships is prolific. He explains,

> Not one Biblical figure was the object of as much love as David. But closer inspection reveals an additional phenomenon: every time the verb 'love' is connected to David's name, the love is directed at him, but does not emanate from him to another.... [T]he verb 'love' is never used to describe *his* relation to anyone.[9]

---

[9] Shalev, *The First and Second Books of Samuel*, ii.

Even in David's emotional lament over Jonathan at his death, "it is so polished and calculating that the reader is liable to think that David is either hiding his emotions or perhaps has none."[10] In David's famous lament, he says,

> I grieve for you, Jonathan my brother;
>> you were very dear to me.
> Your love for me was wonderful,
>> more wonderful than that of women.[11]

David chooses to describe the love of their friendship as "your love for me" rather than more reciprocal language like "our love" or "my love for you."[12] Therefore, while we know David to be very emotionally expressive and vulnerable in many parts of his story,[13] it is clear that Jonathan is the one more willing to express the meaning of his relationship to David.

Jonathan, then, appears to be the primarily nurturer of the relationship. Jonathan is the one who initiates the initial covenant agreement.[14] Later, Jonathan initiates a covenant to the entire house of David,[15] after which the text describes, "Jonathan made David swear again by his love for him, for he loved him as he loved his own soul."[16] Thus, Jonathan appears to be the primary initiator of the relationship, while David receives the most benefit. The benefits are significant, for David is able to survive Saul's plots against him because of Jonathan's actions,[17] which pave the way for David to assume the throne of Israel.[18] In contrast, Jonathan himself feels the wrath of his own father because of his loyalty to David, even leading to an attempt on his life after defending David.[19]

It is not for lack of commitment to the friendship that David relies so heavily on Jonathan's good will to sustain the friendship. David expressed great affection for Jonathan.[20] David certainly is reciprocal in his love for Jonathan and their friendship. Yet, the reality is that for this

---

[10] Shalev, *The First and Second Books of Samuel*, ii.

[11] 2 Samuel 1:26.

[12] Shalev, *The First and Second Books of Samuel*, ii.

[13] David's lament over the death of Absalom (2 Samuel 18:33), his outpouring over the death of his infant son (2 Samuel 12:16), as well as the evocative nature of David's psalms all point to a man willing to express feelings and emotions.

[14] I Samuel 18:3.

[15] I Samuel 20:16.

[16] I Samuel 20:17 (ESV).

[17] I Samuel 20.

[18] I Samuel 23:17.

[19] I Samuel 20:30-34.

[20] I Samuel 20:41.

relationship to have the life it had, Jonathan had to bear a greater cost. David was the needier friend. Not unlike today's pastors who get engulfed by the many responsibilities of their calling, David was continually overwhelmed in the calling placed upon his life. In accepting friendship with David, Jonathan accepted the circumstances involved with befriending the next King of Israel. Jonathan willingly surrendered himself to the relationship, finding meaning in helping his friend rise to the calling placed upon him. So too does the pastor require a friend who can absorb the many sacrifices that are often required to be the pastor's friend.

Lastly, we see in Jonathan and David the way in which a meaningful friendship connects to the survival of ministry. For David, this need for survival is quite literal. Jonathan's friendship meant that David could survive the plots of Saul. One wonders how David would have survived Saul's plots against him if not for the practical interventions of his closest friend. If Jonathan had chosen against David, likely, Jonathan would have attained the throne while David would have died prematurely at the hand of Saul. For David, his friendship with Jonathan produced very practical and life-saving results.

In contrast, one sees how the increasing isolation of Saul mirrors the destruction of his reign. One of the devices of 1 Samuel 18 is that by its end, the hopelessness of Saul's reign has become overwhelmingly evident.[21] David has received the adoration of the crowds, is loved by Saul's daughter, and receives a soul friend in Jonathan. Saul himself is "a remarkably isolated man,"[22] having lost the loyalty and support of those closest to him. We see in David's success and Saul's failures the way in which intimate relationships (or lack thereof) play a part in those successes and failures.

If David's success is connected to the support of his closest friend, and Saul's isolation is symptomatic of his own failing reign, one begins to wonder what successes and failures could be connected to the pastor and the support he or she receives from close friends. David and Jonathan certainly offer up the picture of ideal friendship, but the significance of their friendship goes beyond that. Their relationship reveals a number of important practical reasons why pastors should consider a close friend not simply an added spice to life, but an essential element to ministry success.

Oscillation Theory and the Healing Role of Friendship

To identify friendship as "essential" to ministry success is a rather bold proposition. How then is friendship impact ministry success? If

---

[21] Brueggemann, *First and Second Samuel*, 139.
[22] Shalev, *The First and Second Books of Samuel*, iii.

something about David and Jonathan's friendship sustained David in his divinely ordained rise to the throne, then how so? How might friendship sustain and help the pastor in the fulfillment of his or her calling? It is to these questions that a paradigm may be helpful. Bruce Reed, an Anglican theologian, offers in his book, *The Dynamics of Religion*,[23] observations about the renewal process inherent in people and organizations—a theory he terms The Oscillation Theory—which when applied to the pastor and his ministry and relational life, may be helpful to our understanding of friendship and today's pastors.

The Oscillation Theory describes an ongoing process in which persons unconsciously, or intuitively, move in and out of periods of activity and renewal for the sake of gathering energy for the tasks ahead and to make meaning of the work to come. One might think of it as the ways in which we oscillate between states of "doing" and "being." Reed described it this way:

> For most people, the ordering of everyday life provides regular cycles of oscillation. Each day includes periods when we address ourselves to the problems of living, and periods when we are fed and cared for, relax, reflect and sleep. Similarly, for many, the week and the year provide occasions for more complete disengagement from the problems of living, in the weekend break or annual holiday. It is onto this base-line, with its regularized opportunities for disengagement, that the oscillation demanded by specific challenges and experiences is superimposed.[24]

Reed then offers that oscillation is one's "periodic disengagement to renew contact with a source of meaning and confidence,"[25] adding that "individuals use the actual or imagined presence of another to provide a setting in which they can acknowledge their own weakness and vulnerability, and re-order their view of themselves and their world."[26] Reed offers a few important terms that give us handles for taking hold of his theory. The two states of "acting" and "being" are described as states of *intra-dependence* and *extra-dependence*. In intra-dependence, one engages a state of independent activity while relying on internal resources to accomplish the tasks one has set out to do. This is a state of autonomy and self-sufficiency. Here, a person calls on resources inside herself (intra) to carry out her work.

---

[23] Bruce D. Reed, *The Dynamics of Religion: Process and Movement in Christian Churches* (London: Darton, Longman and Todd, 1978).

[24] Reed, *The Dynamics of Religion*, 15.

[25] Reed, *The Dynamics of Religion*, 13.

[26] Reed, *The Dynamics of Religion*, 19.

121

After a period of intra-dependence, one moves into a state of extra-dependence. In this state, the person retreats from a state of activity towards a state of being, resting, and meaning making. In this state, the person calls on resources outside herself (extra) to provide play, rest, and renewal, so that she may be prepared for re-entry into the intra-dependent state. It is in extra-dependence that a trustworthy and caring person or persons are essential to helping one experience the full renewing capabilities of extra-dependence.

Roy Oswald has written much on the clergy's need for effective self-care and applies Reed's theory as a model for pastors in understanding their own needs for nurture and renewal. The same process that Reed identifies as working in the life of the congregation, Oswald sees working in the life of the pastor. The pastor, too, moves in and out of states of doing and being, self-reliance and dependence, action and reflection.[27] Figure 2, drawn both from Reed and Oswald, illustrates the states of action and being involved in the oscillation process.

THE OSCILLATION PROCESS

INTRA-DEPENDENCE	EXTRA-DEPENDENCE
Doing	Being
Reliance on Self	Reliance on Others
Action	Reflection
Independence	Dependence
Work	Play
Role	Essence
Task Orientation	Sabbath Time
Productivity	Vulnerability
Law	Grace
Uni-directional	Reciprocal
Objective World	Subjective World

Figure 2: Characteristics of the States of
Intra-Dependence and Extra-Dependence[28]

---

[27] Roy M. Oswald, *Clergy Self-Care: Finding a Balance For Effective Ministry* (Washington, DC: Alban Institute, 1991), 130–135.

[28] Drawn from Oswald, *Clergy Self-Care*, 132, and Reed, *The Dynamics of Religion*, 32-34.

A balanced oscillation between states of intra-dependence and extra-dependence is essential to a pastor's personal health. Few can survive while continually operating in the state of intra-dependence, for in that state, pastors are living beneath the requirements of an achievement-oriented culture. In intra-dependence, things are manipulated and people are functioning for the accomplishment of goals. This underscores the need for the periodic immersion into extra-dependence. There, things and people are accepted just as they are. It is a safe environment in which one's playfulness emerges and the "shoulds and oughts" of communal life that are set aside so that we are accepted just the way we are.[29]

Reed offers another observation that informs the renewal needs of the pastor. Reed first applied his observations to Christian worship and the role that the church worship experience plays in nurturing its members. When people enter the life of the church, they enter worship and relationship as a retreat from their own states of intra-dependence in order to find meaning and renewal in the extra-dependent state offered by faith and spirituality. In light of this context, Reed sees religion as "a corporate activity which provides a ritual setting for one of the modes of the oscillation process, the extra-dependent mode, and thereby 'binds together' the lives of those who participate in it."[30] He adds that "in religion… they seek sanction or strength for their lives from outside themselves; it is an extra-dependent mode."[31] Worshipers come together to express their dependence upon one another and upon God through a common set of beliefs and rituals. Therefore, in the oscillation process of independence and dependence, the church functions as the place of meaning making and renewal, preparing believers to actively engage the world in which they work, serve, and live.

The impact on the pastor is significant. For in a gathering of extra-dependent worshippers, the pastor is a central human figure upon which the congregation relies for their renewal. This means that whereas most congregants find the church to be a place of extra-dependence, the pastor finds the church a place of extraordinary intra-dependence. The pastor, as the caregiver and shepherd for a large group of extra-dependent people, bears a significant responsibility for tending to the group's need for renewal and meaning in their lives.

Add to this the fact that persons in the mode of extra-dependence are often in a state of regression based simply on the fact that when persons make themselves vulnerable to the care of others, they retreat to a more "child-like" state of mind, where stories, narratives, images, and

---

[29] Oswald, *Clergy Self-Care*, 131.
[30] Reed, *The Dynamics of Religion*, 50.
[31] Reed, *The Dynamics of Religion*, 50.

other-worldly ideas can germinate.[32] This regression can complicate the pastor's work. If a pastor has ever wondered why a member of the church spends five days a week in a work environment where change and progress are acceptable and expected but then responds quite reactively to minor changes in the order of worship, this may be the reason.[33] The congregational environment acts as a place of safety and retreat away from the affronts and demands of work and community life. As one writer describes it, "We all venture out like children ranging out into the park in play, but from time to time we need to come running back to Mother for renewal. We can then go off running again merrily on our own. Sometimes we need to regress to go forward.[34]" Pastors are tending to this need for regression in those they serve and must do so in a way that nurtures and prepares them for re-entry into the demands of life. What this underscores once again is the intensity of expectation and pressure a pastor feels as he or she leads congregants through this complex renewal of spirit.

This leads us full circle back to the importance of meaningful friendships in the pastor's life. A pastor who tends so profoundly to the extra-dependent needs of so many must herself enter willingly and regularly into the safety of extra-dependent renewal. This is certainly found in a robust and meaningful relationship with God as the faithful giver of life. But it is also found in the tender support of colleagues, family, and friends. Simply put, a pastor who spends great amounts of intra-dependent energy without allowing others to pour renewal, warmth, and affection back into the pastor's well of energy and passion, then that pastor is on the trajectory of exhaustion and burnout.

This moves us closer to the answer to the question, is friendship essential? Perhaps not in the immediate rush of worship planning, sermon preparation, and hospital visitation. But the close friend is essential to the pastor's renewal. Pastors may inadvertently buy into the belief that they possess a superhero-like abundance of intra-dependence

---

[32] Reed, *The Dyncamics of Religion*, 22. Reed recognizes that the word "regression" has negative overtones that suggest dysfunction or infantile behavior. Instead, "regression may be seen as a re-version, not necessarily to the primitive mentality of the infant, but to the unclouded vision of the child; but in either case the process may be repugnant to the adult mind."

[33] One wonders if the pressure pastors often place on congregation members to accept the latest fashions in church programming counteracts the very process of spiritual fortification and renewal congregants require in order to effectively engage the mission of the church in the world. Much of the scramble to be relevant to ever changing cultural whims may itself inflict further trauma upon church members rather than tend to their need for weekly renewal.

[34] Jerome Berryman, *Godly Play: An Imaginative Approach to Religious Education* (Minneapolis, MN: Augsburg Books, 1994), 88.

or that they can depend on "God alone" for their renewal needs to be met. On the contrary, no one is equipped with such depth of internal resources as to neglect their extra-dependent needs for long. The Oscillation Theory resonates with truth, as it speaks to what self-aware pastors know to be true. They cannot continue to spend without being renewed. This means that the pastor's friendships are not simply a touching appendage to their clergy support system. But, in fact, the close friend may offer the greatest hope of extra-dependent renewal for the depleted pastor.

Recommendations to the Pastor

Given the wide array of information that has now been set before us regarding the pastor's friendships, it is important to gather this information together into a few summary recommendations. Again, given that there is so much subjectivity in friendship, it may be pushing the natural limits to offer anything so bold as "final conclusions," for such conclusions will inevitably fall prey to the variability of friendship's many situations and circumstances. However, there are enough consistent experiences offered by the pastors in this study that out of the themes of this project, one can draw recommended action points for the pastor in his or her experience of friendship.

The following recommendations represent this researcher's interpretation of all the data drawn from the academic reading, theological reflection, and the interviews that were integrated into this study. What follows are my conclusions about action that pastors can take to assist them in navigating through the complex world of pastoral relationships and their friendships. These recommendations are unique to the pastor. These are recommendations that, taken out of their pastoral context, would appear odd in most people's experience of friendship. The hope is that pastors will find the outcomes of this study to be practical in their everyday experience of pastoral care and relationship building that is such an integral part of effective congregational ministry.

Recommendation: Make friendship intentional.

Most people will live full and complete lives without ever giving much thought to why and how and to what extent they enjoy friendship. Most will experience the luxuries of friendship unencumbered by concerns about how much self-disclosure is appropriate to the relationship. Nor will many outside the pastoral discipline ever take inventory of how many friends they have, what role those friendships play, or if they are helping or hurting their work life. For the pastor, however, engagement with friendship only on the instinctive level promises unattractive and painful consequences.

Intentionality about the pastor's friendship, then, is a key component of a thoughtful and deliberate pastoral care philosophy. While the pastor trains and prepares for ministry through the interior work of spiritual reflection, scriptural meditation, and prayerful practices, the pastor's public work carries no more essential tool than his or her relatedness to others. It is well known that the pastor with great oratory skills or deep theological or biblical insights who has an impaired ability to relate to others is not long for pastoral life. Pastors impact the lives of others through relationship, whether it is in counseling, at the hospital bedside, or at the church social. Relationships are the vehicle through which pastoral care and influence is transmitted. The importance of these relationships is never more apparent than when those relationships fail. The ripple effect of fractured relationships inflicts a painful blow to the pastor's credibility and effectiveness.

Therefore, any pastor who takes seriously the role and influence of the pastorate ought to maintain a high degree of relational awareness. Certainly, numerous books, conferences, and resources invite the pastor to do just this. There is no shortage of guidance about how to engage the elder board, how to guide sensitive changes within the congregation, or how to provide pastoral care through relational presence. What appears to be absent, however, is intentionality around the relationships with those persons with whom we feel the greatest connection. Beyond the well-worn prohibitions of simply avoiding friendships altogether, few pastors are invited to prepare for their closest relationships and for how those relationships will impact their overall ministry and self-care.

Thus, I invite pastors to be intentional about their friendships. This invitation extends to three areas. The first is to be intentional about how the pastor's role in the congregation affects friendship. The second is to be intentional about how close friendships sustain the pastor through a lifetime of ministry. The last is to be intentional about seeking and forming friendships.

Regarding the first two areas, much has already been said. Pastors who understand how their friendships are affected by the relational dynamics and pastoral expectations within the congregation can then engage their pastoral relationships and friendships with more clarity and confidence. Furthermore, they can then embrace friendship as a significant part of their self-care strategy, welcoming good friendships for what they provide, while also recognizing what the lack of good friendship can mean to the pastor in terms of isolation, fatigue, and burnout. I am hopeful that anyone who has engaged this projected to this point has achieved a high level of awareness about how friendships impact pastoral relationships and how they serve the pastor's personal well-being.

It is the third area of intentionality that requires closer examination. One skill of the thoughtful pastor ought to be the intentional formation and development of friendships. Friendships may occur naturally for many, but it appears that the environment in which pastors live and serve suppress the very natural forces that allow close friendships to emerge. As has been noted, the pastor forms many close relationships throughout a lifetime of pastoral interactions. Yet despite the vast opportunity for close relationships to form, the pastor's role along with the limits of his ability to be deeply vulnerable with congregants taint the soil in which friendship emerges. A friendship may naturally grow towards meaningful intimacy only for the realities of pastoral functioning to cut the relationship short of its fullest potential. And yet to look for that close friendship outside the church, where intimacy has far fewer hindrances, one is challenged by the time that it takes to nurture those relationships effectively.

To choose to be intentional about forming friendship is to refuse to surrender to these realities. Many a pastor has no doubt lamented their lack of close friendships only to accept that this is the price of the pastorate or "our calling to the sacrificial loneliness of leadership."[35] With eyes open to the renewing potential of friendships inside and outside the church, one may gain a greater resolve to restructure a schedule or follow up a lead or delegate away a time-consuming responsibility in order to create time to nurture friendships.

To say that friendship formation ought to be an intentional process for the pastor is not to say that friendship can be forced. No matter how much one may seek the friendship of another, the connection of two people to each other is at some level an inexplicable process. What one can be intentional about is battling against the obstacles of time and challenging circumstances to make it possible for friendship to take root. It may be that the time sacrifices involved in nurturing such relationships could have enough rejuvenating effect as to make the pastor's limited time more productive. As one pastoral care expert offered,

> If a minister really values friendship and desires friends, he will need to set priorities that allow appropriate time for developing these relationships. He will not give in too quickly when he meets obstacles to ministerial friendships, but will creatively diminish some of the roadblocks' force.[36]

---

[35] Benjamin D. Schoun, "Can a Pastor Have Friends?" *Ministry: International Journal for Clergy* (July 1986): 8.

[36] Schoun, "Can a Pastor Have Friends?" 9.

Therefore, to be intentional about friendship in no way undermines the natural forces that make a friendship truly flourish. It only helps them begin.

Along these lines, social psychologist, Steve Duck, in his book, *Friends for Life*,[37] reminds us that every friend was once a stranger to us, and that despite what we may think, "[R]elationships do not just happen; they have to be made—made to start, made to work, made to develop, kept in good working order and preserved from going sour."[38] Therefore, it is a fallacy to think that friendships will simply arrive without effort. In fact, the potential close friend may be a stranger at present and requires our intentional efforts to give the relationship the hope of possibility.

This is where Duck and others[39] can be a helpful to any pastor willing to invest time and effort into building friendships. His book offers strategies for starting, nurturing, and developing friendships and for acquiring the necessary skills to maintain these relationships. For example, he describes a common error in friendship development that prevents many potential friendships from forming. Many believe that factors such as attraction and common interest are the fundamental basis of friendship formation. If those initial connections are not made and attraction is not present, the relationship is discounted as a potential friendship. Duck says that this belief oversimplifies the complexities of friendship and minimizes the essential work that is required for healthy and meaningful relationships to form:

> A relationship has to be created and forged jointly by testing the likelihood that it will work, assessing and displaying trust (and the other person's trustworthiness), sharing of secrets, development of intimacy, confidence in another's advice, organization of daily life together, and emotional support in times of trouble. These must all be allowed to take time to surface in a relationship and cannot be rushed.[40]

The contemporary notion that friendships happen naturally without much effort by two people who feel a mysterious connection fails to appreciate the effort required in relationship building. Furthermore, it misses out on the meaningful friendships that could arise should two people choose to invest in their relationship.

---

[37] Steve Duck, *Friends, For Life: The Psychology of Personal Relationships*, 2nd ed. (New York: Harvester Wheatsheaf, 1991).

[38] Duck, *Friends, For Life: The Psychology of Personal Relationships*, 3.

[39] See Beverley Fehr, *Friendship Processes* (Thousand Oaks, CA: Sage Publications, 1996), 43-69 for her practical insights on friendship-making.

[40] Duck, *Friends, For Life: The Psychology of Personal Relationships*, 29–30.

Duck further adds, "Similarities are obviously discovered and demonstrated bit by bit. Initially the two attracted partners can only suspect that they are similar, but later the delightful commonalities are extensively discovered during the process of acquaintance."[41] In other words, judging the potential of a friendship based on initial impressions might be to judge its potential without the proper information. Such superficial judgment may cause one to overlook a relationship that may be rich with deeper commonalities that await discovery.

Rather than judging a potential friendship on first impressions, common interests or natural forces, the pastor can practice intentionality by engaging a potential friend with a test of appropriate self-disclosure. Emory Griffin offers a metaphor that illustrates how a pastor might negotiate the self-disclosure involved in making friends, describing the delicacy of a pastor's self-disclosure as a turtle emerging from his shell:

> Picture two turtles—face to face—with their heads almost completely hidden. One turtle extends his neck just a bit. If the other turtle responds in kind, then the first one ventures out some more. In a series of minute movements the first turtle ends up with his head in the sunshine, but only if his counterpart follows his lead. At any time he's prepared to slow the progression, come to a complete stop, or even back off.[42]

Like our metaphorical turtle, the pastor can judge the potential of a friendship through patient and careful risk taking.[43] Griffin writes, the pastor "takes the initial risk. He's always a tad ahead of the game-testing, probing, hoping. But at the same time he's constantly monitoring the other's response and is ready to pull back when confronted with indifference or hostility."[44]

Beverly Fehr, in addressing friendship formation, speaks of self-disclosure this way:

> [I]f each interaction is rewarding (has a positive outcome), we will continue to increase both the breadth and depth of our disclosures until we are revealing virtually everything about ourselves on virtually every topic. If, however, the exchange of disclosures becomes uncomfortable or unpleasant, we will retreat to our earlier, more superficial and circumscribed mode of self-disclosure.[45]

---

[41] Duck, *Friends, For Life: The Psychology of Personal Relationships*, 30.
[42] Griffin, "Self-Disclosure: How Far Should a Leader Go?," 130.
[43] Griffin, "Self-Disclosure: How Far Should a Leader Go?," 130.
[44] Griffin, "Self-Disclosure: How Far Should a Leader Go?," 130.
[45] Fehr, *Friendship Processes*, 63.

She further adds that self-disclosure "signals a desire to develop closeness," meaning that the act of careful self-disclosure is a significant way of being intentional in testing the possibility of friendship.[46] Fehr adds that "there are limits to this effect. For example, if someone we have just met discloses highly intimate information to us, we might feel uncomfortable and not be attracted to the person."[47] Timing, she says, is the key. A friendship must begin with superficial levels of self-disclosure and gradually take on more intimate exchanges of information.[48] One way to gauge the reception of self-disclosing information is the nature of the other's response. In self-disclosing conversations, "friends engage in more behaviors [that] continue and sustain the conversation,"[49] asking more questions and providing lengthier responses to what they are hearing. A potential friend will be less likely to disagree, will express more interest, and laugh more.[50] Awareness of these factors can help a pastor determine whether to retreat back into their metaphorical shell or to move carefully into greater self-disclosure.

Beyond self-disclosure, it appears that the situational environment or context of the relationship is crucial to the friendship formation. To be intentional about forming friendships, the relationship may require moving to a different environment than the relationship's usual context. Duck illustrates this in his study of co-workers who were invited to meet in an environment outside of work. This change of environment changed the relationship. "The differences between work and play seem to the unskilled eye to matter very little. In fact, they are, on the contrary, extremely significant in relationships, not because of what they *are* but because of how they make people see one another."[51] Sometimes, a simple change in environment can reveal traits about a person that may not have been discovered otherwise.[52]

---

[46] Fehr, *Friendship Processes*, 63.

[47] Fehr, *Friendship Processes*, 63.

[48] Fehr, *Friendship Processes*, 63. Fehr also points to studies that show that timing of self-disclosure is important not only over time, but in the timing of a specific conversation. "There is evidence that a person is better liked when he or she discloses intimate information late, rather than early, in a conversation."

[49] Fehr, *Friendship Processes*, 86. Fehr adds that persons who are growing in their friendship will not only responds with more complex and inquisitive questioning about a particular self-disclosure, but will initiate other topics of self-disclosure.

[50] Fehr, *Friendship Processes*, 87.

[51] Duck, *Friends, For Life: The Psychology of Personal Relationships*, 37.

[52] Ray Pahl, *On Friendship* (Malden, MA: Polity Press, 2000), 131-132. This can happen with reverse effect. Pahl points out that once a relationship leaves its initial context, social and economic realities that were once transcended in the original context now become influential factors in the viability of the friendship. A change of environment may reveal that there are too many differences to sustain the friendship.

One way, then, that pastors can take initiative in friendship formation is to meet potential friends outside the usual ministry setting. If one sees a pastoral colleague regularly at a denominational meeting, the relationship will have its limits in that setting. To meet that pastor on the golf course or to invite that pastor and his spouse over for dinner may create an atmosphere where attractive personal traits can come to light. While this does not guarantee the relationship grows into life-long friendship, it does create the space for that possibility. No doubt, as this becomes an intentional practice for a pastor, that there will be an increase in the number of meaningful friendships that will be formed over time.

James, a pastor in our study, shared about meaningful friendships that were formed out of his intentional efforts. When he moved into his neighborhood, he and his wife would walk the newly built neighborhood praying expectantly that Christian people might move into their neighborhood. Each time a new house was built and a new neighbor moved in, he and his wife would make efforts to welcome them and introduce themselves. James said that this had a transformational effect on him as a new world of friendships opened up to him. He describes his Catholic neighbors who they share meals with and are able to relate to outside of his role as pastor. James stated that he is very aware of how different these friendships are from those inside his congregation. James offered that an interesting reflection. When he thinks about ever relocating to a new church, he realizes, "I'll miss my neighbors more than I miss my congregation."[53] These relationships have had a grounding effect on James and his wife, as they give them a connection to the community beyond their own church. The loss of these friendships will one day be a factor in any decision to move to another congregation.

Despite the potential benefits of an intentional approach towards friendship formation, it is of interest that James was the only one of the ten pastors who described making intentional efforts to develop friendships outside of his congregation. Intentional relationship building outside of the many relationships a pastor is involved with may seem overwhelming or even unnecessary. In fact, pastors often struggle with relationship fatigue and find no need for developing *more* relationships. One writer described a conversation with a tired pastor who felt pressed to his limits, "'I'm around people all the time. I don't need people. I need peace.'"[54] The Theological Colloquium from Duke University found that among a focus group of pastors, the pastors ranked their need for friends far below their need for other relationships in their lives, namely "mentors and confidants, people with whom they could feel safe

---

[53] "James." Interview with author. October 3, 2013.
[54] Schoun, "Can a Pastor Have Friends?" 9.

confiding their flaws, people who could hold them accountable and contribute to their spiritual formation." The writer insightfully noted, "The very things clergy said they wanted—mentoring accountability, and spiritual formation—are inherent in the kinds of friendship the colloquium described [as helpful to pastors]."[55]

It is evident, then, that for many pastors, the decision to add new relationships to the many that already call for the pastor's attention might seem taxing. But as pastors assess their own relational needs, they may find that these additional efforts may bring a renewal that will not only meet their own relational needs, but may bring fuel for the many relational duties that are so a part of pastors' every day work.

Recommendation: Take personal inventory of relational needs and the friends who fill them.

Once committed to an intentional approach to friendship, the next step is to assess one's own relational needs and the friendship resources capable of meeting those needs. The key questions are, in what areas is the pastor soundly supported by good friends and where is the pastor left vulnerable to isolation and loneliness? In answering these questions, it is important for the pastor to devote the time and effort to writing out a complete list of friends. The act of writing out this list is a critical discipline for the pastor. The undertaking helps the pastor focus intently on who provides the most personal significance to the pastor in his relationships. It aids the pastor in calling to mind the support that is around him. This assessment enables the pastor to identify gaps in her extra-dependent support and where she is susceptible to personal isolation. The pastor might be able, then, to anticipate weaknesses in his or her support system and direct proper energies towards filling those relational needs.

For the list to be most helpful, it is important that the list be broad. Such a list should include a wide range of friends, from beloved acquaintances to the very closest of friends. The list should reflect friends from a wide variety of contexts, including one's current ministry setting, educational settings of the past, former congregations, one's denominational network, one's immediate community or neighborhood, etc. The intent of such a broad list is to help not only identify current friends, but potential ones as well. With an intentional eye focused on these important relationships, it may be that one will identify acquaintances who hold the potential of becoming a close friend.

With this list hand, the next step is to assess how these friendships connect to one's relational needs. Where is the strongest support? Where

---

[55] Bob Wells, "Friendship: It's Okay to Go There," *Divinity* 2, no. 2 (Winter 2003): 4.

FRIENDSHIP TYPES

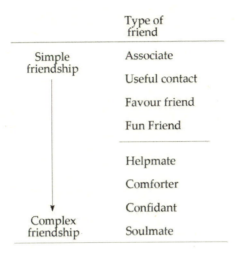

Figure 3: Spencer and Pahl's Recurrent Friendship Types[56]

are there gaps? Spencer and Pahl can be helpful to us in this regard. In their book, *Rethinking Friendship*, they have carefully identified eight friendship types (see figure 3).   The description of these types reveals basic relational needs that friends fill. In the eight friendship types, they are divided into two basic categories, those being simple and complex friendships. Simple friends have "one main form of interaction."[57] These friendships are based on a primary function and could be described as functional friendships. These are along the lines of what Aristotle called friendships of utility and pleasure. They meet basic relational needs of cordiality, helpfulness, recreation, basic support and kindness. Looking at simple friendships, Spencer and Pahl write,

> In simple friendships, friends play well-defined and somewhat circumscribed roles. The friends may be *associates* who share a common activity, *useful contacts* who exchange information and advice, *neighbourly* or *favour friends* who help each other out, or *fun friends* who socialize together. Of course, other friendships also involve fun and favours, but the key feature of simple friendships is that the relationship is limited to one main form of interaction. [58]

---

[56] Spencer and Pahl, *Rethinking Friendship*, 60.

[57] Liz Spencer and Ray Pahl, *Rethinking Friendship: Hidden Solidarities Today* (Princeton, NJ: Princeton University Press, 2006), 60.

[58] Spencer and Pahl, *Rethinking Friendship*, 60.

Two friends in this kind of relationship might connect through a form of recreation, or through help on a job, or through a shared interest in a hobby. The simple friend, however, may not have other qualities, like trustworthiness or reliability or other types of personal qualities to move the relationship beyond the friendship's basic function.[59] Simple friendships capture a vast number of what we call friends. Even the loneliest pastor may find themselves with no shortage of simple friends.

A complex friendship, on the other hand, is one in which the friend crosses from a single form of interaction to "several different ways of relating."[60] These are the multi-faceted friendships that move beyond a single role and meet more complex relational needs. In their more complex roles, these friends are the ones we feel comfortable turning to for emotional, not just functional support. This friendship transcends the simple function out of which it was first formed.

One gets a sense of when a simple friendship begins to become complex. Spencer and Pahl describe the transition. "[Friends] wonder whether to put themselves forward, whether it is 'that kind of friendship,' whether it would be presumptuous on their part."[61] Furthermore, "people sometimes make subtle calculations about the strength of a friendship in relation to the kind of help being requested."[62] One sees that as a friendship begins to move into a more complex form, two people begin to test the relationship by allowing increased expectations to be placed upon the relationship. If the friendship can absorb these new expectations, a deeper connection begins to be formed, allowing opportunity for greater emotional and relational needs to be met.

It is in complex friendships that the pastor requires the most intentionality and awareness. It is here that levels of vulnerability will be tested and can potentially come into conflict with the pastoral role. It is here, too, that the pastor may notice her greatest relationship void, for these healthy, complex friendships are often the most difficult to form and maintain in the pastorate. When those complex friends are inside the church, these friends may only be able to go so far down the road of intimacy. They may be able to perform well as helpmates or comforters, but may be limited by the pastor's role to serve as confidants or soulmates. As a pastor reflects upon his list of friends, it is important to ask how many of his complex friendships are able to serve at these higher levels. A pastor may have meaningful complex friends, but may

---

[59] Spencer and Pahl, *Rethinking Friendship*, 60.
[60] Spencer and Pahl, *Rethinking Friendship*, 60.
[61] Spencer and Pahl, *Rethinking Friendship*, 67.
[62] Spencer and Pahl, *Rethinking Friendship*, 66.

determine through a friendship inventory that he is missing the kind of higher level friendships that will sustain him through ministry.

Pastoral Friendship Types

Building on these friendship types, I offer my own paradigm. This paradigm flows out of my reflections on the interviews and research on pastors and their friendship. Borrowing from Spencer and Pahl's concept of friendship types and complexity, I seek to reframe these friendship types in order to put them in line with what we know about the unique complexities of the pastor's ministry environment. In this paradigm (see figure 4), I offer four friendship types the pastor is likely to experience. These friendship types are connected to two significant factors affecting the pastor's friendships, those being the pastor's need for vulnerability and the congregation's expectation from the pastoral role.

The first and most basic friendship is the *Role Friend*. It carries this name to remind the pastor that in this friendship, the pastoral role still is primary. The friendship qualities that do exist endure only as the breadth of the pastoral role integrity is able to allow it. Because the traditional role of the pastor remains fully intact, there is a correspondingly low threshold of vulnerability. Any expressions of vulnerability that appear to go against the expected role undermine the pastor's effectiveness.

This friendship type identifies a majority of the friendships that pastors enjoy within their congregations. These friends are a significant source of joy for the pastor and can make pastoring a pleasure, as people engage the pastor on both on friendly and pastoral terms. This kind of friendship is an asset to the pastor, as it in enables the pastor to provide a more personal level of pastoral care and leadership. Pastors who foster very few of these friendships are likely to be thought of as too aloof or distant, causing relational barriers between the people and pastor. Thus, this friendship flows out of the inherently personal nature of pastoral care and is itself a help in the pastoral ministry.

It is at this level of friendship, however, that the pastor must be aware of the limits of the relationship. While pastoral friends at this level express themselves in very friendly terms, they continue to relate primarily to the pastor according to the pastoral role. When vulnerability and role collide, these friends expect the role to come first. Any vulnerability that would undermine the pastoral role is expected to be held in silence. The bottom line of the Role Friend is that the friendship lies secondary to the pastor's main responsibility as spiritual leader.

FRIENDSHIP TYPE	VULNERABILITY LEVEL	ROLE EXPECTATION	FRIENDSHIP FUNCTIONS	EXAMPLES
ROLE FRIEND	**Restrained** Friendship is present but remains secondary to my pastoral role.	**High** Expressions of vulnerability potentially undermine pastoral relationship	Contextualized friendship Practical Help Recreation Small favors Casual	Social church friends Recreational Friends Congregation members
	Characteristics: The Role Friendship develops from the congeniality of the pastor/parishioner relationship. Pastors must be aware that the pastoral role is primary and that the friendship can tolerate only minimal expressions of vulnerability.			
CIVIC FRIEND	**Restrained** Friendship develops out of a common purpose, but is secondary to the mission.	**Complex** Pastoral role can absorb increased vulnerability that emerges from shared vision and purpose	Advantage Friendship Shared vision High relational investment Confidant Emotional support	Church elders Church leaders Fellow clergy Colleagues/ Church staff Deacons Committee leaders
	Characteristics: The Civic Friendship develops from a shared vision. when working together on a shared vision. Pastors must be aware that the loyalties of the friendship are often secondary to loyalties to the institution.			

CLOSE FRIEND	**Moderate** I can share almost anything about myself and still honor my pastoral role.	**Complex** Reasonable levels of vulnerability enhances the pastoral relationship	Helpmate Confidant Emotional Support Affection Companionship	Church leader friends Recreational friends Staff friendships Fellow Clergy
Characteristics: The Close Friendship rises out of the natural attraction principles of friendship and allows more vulnerability to be present in the pastoral role. Pastors must be aware that pastoral role expectations continue to limit full expressions of vulnerability.				
IDEAL FRIEND	**Maximum** I can share anything about myself and expect to feel safe and accepted.	**None** Vulnerability is disconnected from pastoral role	Confidant High levels of acceptance and trust Close affection Commitment Transcends time & place	Usually outside congregation Lifelong friend Childhood friend College/Seminary Former church Member Fellow Clergy
Characteristics: The Ideal Friendship is the most intimate of friendships where the pastoral role has no impact on the range of vulnerability that can be expressed.				

Figure 4: Pastoral Friendship Types

The second friendship type is the *Civic Friend*. This friendship type, which is quite common in pastoral life, flows out of the work in chapter three in which we identified the complex relational components involved in maintaining close relationships with those in church leadership. Pastors commonly develop close relationships with those with whom they share leadership. After all, these are often the people who most understand the pastor's vision for the church and share the same love for the church's mission. Because of the common goals and interests that are associated with working together on a shared mission, it is natural for meaningful friendships to form out of this work.

Let it be acknowledged that the term "civic friend" does not capture the spiritual nature of church leadership like one would hope. In fact, the term "civic friend" was chosen not because it perfectly captures the concept, but because of a lack of better alternatives. This friendship type has been popularized in other disciplines with words like "political friendship" or "advantage friendship," but these terms have connotations that cheapen friendship into something manipulative. Certainly that is not what we are describing here with the civic friendship. Sadly, no term has been developed to describe the close friendships in church life that rise out of working together in church leadership.

Ultimately, the challenge of civic friendships is that they often appear as the kind of close friendships where high levels of vulnerability and self-disclosure are welcome. Much personal energy is given to these relationships. However, the civic friendship has an interesting caveat, in that the relationship has a higher value in view. For the civic friend, the advancement of the institution, or in this case, the church, takes priority over the friendship. This friendship may be very personal, but it is highly functional at the same time. The friendship functions to gather good will in such a way that the purposes of the church can be advanced. Hence, a pastor commonly develops a close friendship with his or her church elders or leaders as they advance a shared mission.

However, as we identified in chapter three, when disagreement arises about how to fulfill that vision, or if it becomes clear that a particular leadership deficit in the pastor threatens the fulfillment of that vision, the loyalties to the institution will often overshadow the personal loyalties that have developed in the friendship. In fact, much of the greatest hurt and pain a pastor experiences comes when a close friend in leadership stands against the pastor alongside others who oppose him. But such is the nature of the civic friendship, and it is worth being aware of how this particular friendship can nurture the pastor and how it can wound him. To name this reality up front in the friendship may serve to mitigate some of the personal pain that will certainly arise if the friendship cracks under the weight of institutional pressures.

One thing to note is that the civic friendship has great potential to change into other friendship types, especially as leadership roles change or diminish. A church leader, for instance, may choose to step aside from a leadership position, enabling the pastor to engage further in friendship activities without the complications of leadership decision-making. Or the friendship may regress into that of a role friend once the common work of leadership is removed from the relationship. Yet, it is also possible that a strong civic friend may develop into a special friendship at a later time, perhaps when the pastor is no longer in leadership at the church.

The third friendship type is the *Close Friend*. This type is much more complex in nature and is characterized by the fact that the pastor continues to relate to this friend in the pastoral role, but the role is reframed in a way that allows high levels of vulnerability between the pastor and the friend. This vulnerability does not threaten the pastoral relationship or the friendship. Unlike the civic friend, the close friend chooses personal loyalty over institutional loyalty. Thus, the pastor's closeness and openness as a human being aids the spiritual development of the friend, enabling the pastor's friendship to flow nicely with his or her pastoral leadership obligation to the friend.

These friendships are a lifeline for the highly-stressed pastor, as he or she looks to these friends for comfort and support in times of difficulty. These are often friends who can accept the pastor on more intimate and personal terms, accept him "as he is" and hear the pastor's frustrations and challenges and bear them appropriately. These friends can offer validation in times of trouble and lend their caring support, honest appraisal, and personal encouragement. These are friends who may well remain faithfully at the pastor's side during a ministry breakdown where the pastor's ministry mistakes have brought about the issues at hand. While mistakes in ministry may mean the friendship of a Role Friend is damaged, it may draw the Close Friend even closer.

But as was noted in the chapter on friendships inside the church, as highly valuable as these friendships are and as sustaining as they ultimately can be, these friendships often have boundaries that prevent the pastor from being as fully open as he or she would be with their closest friend. These are the friendships that have the most potential to remain with the pastor after he has left the pastoral role and thus become a life-long friend. These are potentially, however, the friendships that may backfire on the pastor, if he or she wrongly interprets how much vulnerability the relationship can bear. The pastor may at a time of vulnerability express something deeply honest within himself that a close friend is not able to receive. This is why many pastors in our study expressed both appreciation and guardedness with these friendships. For it is with these friends that a pastor exercises the most risk.

Finally, we have the *Ideal Friend*. This is the friend who is able, without reservation, to bear the full personhood of the pastor, despite what complexities and intricacies about the pastor might be revealed. These are the friends whose love and acceptance transcends situations and seasons of ministry. These are the ones who know the pastor as they are beyond her position and role. These, in fact, may not think of the pastor as pastor at all, but simply as friend. These are the ones who the pastor knows he can turn to in the best and worst of times, for this is the friend who will no doubt receive him without condition. This friend is a willing co-bearer of a pastor's pain, joy, doubts, and dilemmas. This is the friend we might imagine when we think of all we hope for in a friend.

As has already been acknowledged, this is the most challenging relationship for the pastor to form. These are the friendships that pastors desire most and yet are least likely to find within their current context of ministry. These are the friendships that the pastor has little time to seek or nourish outside the church. However, these are the friendships that could play the most significant role in the pastor's personal support system. It is the central dilemma identified in this project.

This leads us back to the significance of intentionality and the value of a friendship inventory. The thoughtful pastor must ask, who are my friends and what role do they play in my ministry? The recommendation at hand is that pastors take time to develop a written list of friends and began to ask, what categories of friends do I have and what friends do I lack? What follows then is to ask, what people in my life have I overlooked who have the potential to become a new friend or to move from a Role Friend to a Close Friend, or a Close Friend to an Ideal Friend? Who do I have to turn to in times of my greatest need? Who can I trust to bear the full reality of who I am?

Once a pastor has identified his or her network of friends and has determined what needs they fill or fail to fill, the pastor is then able to think intentionally about a strategy for creating fertile soil on which the seeds of new friendships are able to grow. It may be to invite a simple friend to engage outside of the traditional context. It may be to initiate more connections with a current friend. It may be to reach out to an old friend from a past congregation and rekindle that friendship. It may be to hear from close friends what your role of pastor means to them, allowing you to share with them what their friendship means to you. With creativity and intention, the thoughtful and aware pastor can take action in his or her relational life to marshal the support he or she needs.

Recommendation: Seek out a network of friends in the absence of a "full service" friend.

It became clear through the process of the research and interviews that pastors engage friendship differently than people of other professions and walks of life. The most significant difference is this: pastors are rarely able to develop and experience a complete friend. The *Ideal Friend* may be a hope that is never realized within the gritty reality of the pastor's world. The challenges of previous chapters—namely limits of time and opportunity, limits of self-disclosure and vulnerability, and the high expectations of the pastoral role—will not miraculously fade away to make more room for friendships to form. It is possible the pastor may commit to intentionally seeking out new friendships only to find the complete friend exists beyond his grasp. Perhaps, pastoral realities will never stop working against it.

Do pastors give up hope of finding a "full service friend?"[63] Are pastors fated to bear their deepest relational needs alone? The pastors in our study exhibited a strong resilience in the absence of a complete friend. While few were able to identify an Ideal Friend, most pastors were able to identify a rich life of friendships. What is working for these pastors? It is found in the fact that healthy pastors form many specialized friendships that together meet the relational needs traditionally filled by a full service friend.

Thus, it is my recommendation that pastors draw upon a broad network of friends to meet relational needs typically met by a single, ideal friend. The pastor's schedule almost requires it. As we have seen, the friendships where the pastor has the most boundaries in place are with those he or she sees most often (friends inside the church). Yet those friends who enable the pastor to step out of role and exhibit the most vulnerability and self-disclosure (childhood friends, friends from former churches, etc.) are friends he or she sees much less often. Furthermore, whereas someone of another profession may have a much smaller circle of relationships in which they can invest much time in few people, the pastor's range of relationships is inherently wide. The pastor has many relationships that each are allowed limited time. The idea of a wide network of friends meets this relational reality for the pastor.

A pastor, then, must develop the skill of calling upon the appropriate friend to meet the pastor's immediate and specific relational need. Our pastors described having a wide range of friends and associates. Each friend may play his or her own specific role in the pastor's friendship needs. A fellow pastor may hear our gripes and concerns. A church elder

---

[63] This effectively descriptive term comes from Schoun, "Can a Pastor Have Friends?," 9.

might dream with us about what the church could become. A childhood friend might bless us with much needed out-of-role time. A trusted Bible study partner might consider our doubts and theological uncertainties with us. A denominational friend might wrestle with us about when it is right to consider another place of ministry. A former church member might bless us with a long weekend away. Another set of friends might regularly lunch with us to help us get our minds off of our daily tasks. A seminary friend might listen empathically to the cost of ministry to our marriages and families.

This is where the friendship inventory is helpful. It enables the pastor to connect certain friends to certain needs that arise in the pastor's life. It does not mean that pastors set out to treat friends as objects for meeting selfish needs. It is to remind pastors who they have in their lives to support them. A number of pastors in our study recalled suffering through pastoral difficulties alone, wishing only after the fact that they had reached out to a friend for support. With an awareness of which friends best meet certain needs, the pastor is more likely to resist the draw towards isolation in a time of anxiety and crisis and engage the appropriate friend.

The pastor would not be unusual in practicing this style of relating. In fact, the idea of a network of friends[64] may already be a cultural reality for many as our society becomes more and more fragmented. Spencer and Pahl speak to the loss in contemporary life of "place-based communities," which describe the rural communities of "pre-modern world…where people knew their place in society and social relationships were based on people's position in the family, their sex, age and trade."[65] The rise of urban centers has undermined place-based community life, "especially in light of apparently ever greater levels of geographic mobility, the process of globalization, and in particular, the spread of new information technologies."[66] This has led, some have argued, to the rise of differentiated friendships where people only reveal parts of themselves to their friends, who they connect to in certain particular contexts.[67] Many a social scientist has expressed concern over "a perceived

---

[64] Spencer and Pahl, *Rethinking Friendship*, 43–46. The authors prefer the term "personal community" over "network" for fear that "the popular notion of networking seems to amount to little more than adding social contacts to an address book." They describe a personal community is "a specific subset of people's informal social relationships--those who are important to them at the time… and include bonds which give both structure and meaning to their lives."

[65] Spencer and Pahl, *Rethinking Friendship*, 11.

[66] Spencer and Pahl, *Rethinking Friendship*, 11.

[67] Spencer and Pahl, *Rethinking Friendship*, 13.

deterioration in social relations, problems of isolation, loneliness, unhappiness and fleeting, transient ties."[68]

Therefore, society at large is facing similar fragmentation with regards to family, friendships and relationships. The community of relationships in which a person lives, works and establishes his or her identity is continually evolving as he or she progresses through various life stages. As the network continues to change, we related to different friends in different ways and in different contexts, adding to the fragmentation. As one sociologist put it, "We play tennis with one friend, watch football with another and share a school run with another."[69] This kind of categorization is increasingly common to friendship in the contemporary context. Therefore, the pastor may tap into any angst he or she may be feeling to identify with congregants who may also be struggling to have their friendship needs met.

In the end, however, this is a reality that pastors in their lives and ministry they cannot afford to overlook. The pastor who laments the absence of really close or ideal friends may in fact have within his reach the kinds of friends who are capable of meeting more relational needs that the pastor originally imagined. No doubt the presence of ideal, complete friends fulfills the pastor's relational longing in a way that a network of friends may never be able to do. Having a large network of friends does not mean the pastor lives in denial of a deeper need. Nor does it mean that a pastor should not hope to develop an ideal friend. The development of a network of friendships is about fulfilling a functional need for the pastor to have certain trusted people to companion with her through the various times of need that go with the many complicated facets of pastoral ministry.

God blesses pastors with many relationships–as demanding as they sometimes are–so as to care for us in times of need. Paul, the Apostle, held a high awareness of this and accessed a host of various friends to meet his complex needs. Paul lists "dear friends" and fellow "brothers and sisters" in the conclusion to his letter to the Romans and commends them for different ways they contributed to his life and ministry.[70] Paul identifies "the only Jews who are my co-workers" as "a comfort to me."[71]

---

[68] Spencer and Pahl, *Rethinking Friendship*, 13.

[69] Pahl, *On Friendship*, 75. Pahl is summarizing the view of 19th century sociologist, Georg Simmel who held strongly that modernity would produce highly differentiated friendships. Simmel imagined the only person one could have close relationship with would be the spouse. Pahl wonders if this contributes to the high rate of divorce. The spouse becomes the only complete friend, and when the spouse is unable to meet the demands of the role, spouses begin "seeking better friends elsewhere."

[70] Romans 16.

[71] Colossians 4:11.

Paul describes a time when he was experiencing great conflict and weariness, only to find the comfort of Titus to be God's means of "comforting the downcast."[72] Paul pleads with the church at Philemon's home to welcome the former slave, Onesimus. In a play on words (Onesimus means *useful*), Paul describes this formerly "useless" man as "my very heart," "my son," who is "very dear to me," and "useful" to Paul in bringing the comfort he was unable to receive from the church while separated from them.[73] When Paul was unable to receive the support of the Philippian church, he received the care of Epaphroditus, who "risked his life" to care for Paul's needs. Paul describes the "sorrow upon sorrow" he would have experienced should Epaphroditus have died in the completion of his mission.[74]

The nature of Paul's life and ministry foreshadows the life and ministry of all who chose to follow the path of congregational care and leadership. It means there will be times of dislocation, opposition, heavy-heartedness, fulfillment, joy, and a wide range of other emotions and experiences. Just as Paul willingly made himself vulnerable to the assistance of so many who offered him care and support to sustain him through an intense life of ministry, so too must pastors lean on a wide range of friends to support him through the many challenges ministry will certainly bring. And just as Paul was able to see the interpersonal support in these functional helpmates, so too must the pastor open wide her eyes to see the interpersonal support that lay before her in the form of co-workers in the faith. The pastor's circle of friends may never be complete, but the intentional pastor committed to taking that extra step in his or her personal relationships may well find the right friend to meet the right need at just the right time.

The Line of Optimal Balance

To bring to a close the recommendations I have set before the reader, I offer the following chart (see figure 5) as a visual means of considering all that we have examined thus far. It functions as a visual map of the pastor's relational world. It seeks to capture the complexities of that world so as to help the pastor visualize way in which friends intersect the pastor's role and relational needs.

To get the full impact of the chart, one begins by noting the two lines that denote the pastor's role expectations and vulnerable in relationship, which each move from low to high. The four friendship types, therefore, have been plotted along this chart to visually note how

---

[72] 2 Corinthians 7:5-7.
[73] Philemon 8-16.
[74] Philippians 2:25-30.

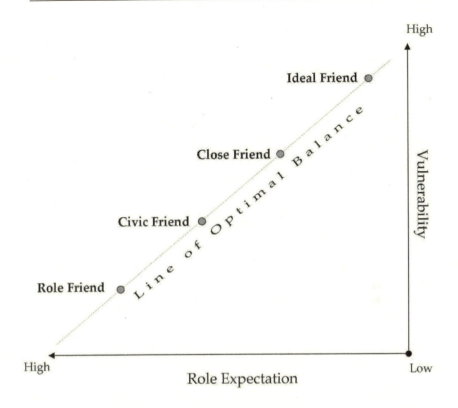

Figure 5: Vulnerability and Role Expectation Scale
for Pastoral Friendship Types

each friendship type corresponds to the expectations of the pastor and the pastor's need to be vulnerable in relationship. One can see, for instance, that the Role Friend sits low on the Vulnerability line, but high on the Role Expectation line. As each relationship becomes more acceptable of vulnerability, role expectations lessen. The four friendship types move along a line that I call the "line of optimal balance." This line marks the critical balance between role expectation and vulnerability that must be held properly in order for healthy friendship to form and thrive.

This chart helps the pastor think about the pastoral and personal relationships that fill his or her life. As the pastor relates to people in his sphere of influence, is he maintaining the right balance between vulnerability and role expectation? When is he able to increase that vulnerability? Has the congregant eased his or her pastoral expectations appropriate to the pastor's expression of vulnerability? If the pastor were to pinpoint her friends on the chart, would she identify a wide enough array friendships so as to fill the length of the line of optimal balance? Do any of those friendships stray too far from the line? Does the pastor need to alter his or her engagement with certain friends in order to bring the relationship back into balance?

These questions are aimed at promoting thought and intentionality. To stray far from the line is to welcome hurt and injury for the pastor as friends are unable to tolerate the complexities of the relationship. Just as important is the damage it inflicts on congregants who expect their pastor to maintain a certainly level of professionalism and thus loses a spiritual authority in their lives when that line is crossed. Therefore, the intentionality promoted throughout these recommendations is not only about intentionally seeking out friends and associating them with specific relational needs. It is also about intentionally maintaining the relational balance that promotes the most effective ministry possible for both the pastor and the congregant.

The Spirituality of Friendship

The goal of this project has been to shine a light on a significant relationship within the life of the pastor that has powerful effect on the pastor's well-being and ministry effectiveness. We began by absorbing the weight of the many expectations on the pastor and the importance of a healthy personal support system. We looked at the many benefits of friendship as a factor in this support system, but came also to the realization that expectations of the pastoral role often conflict with the goals of friendship, which are openness and authenticity which come about through self-disclosure and vulnerability. By enlisting the voices of current-day pastors, we were able to glean insights into how pastors manage these complexities. Essentially, we learned that pastors have rich friendships inside the church but acknowledge that they can only go so far in those friendships while in the congregational context.

We also learned that pastors have meaningful friendships beyond the church environment, and that these friendships provide a way for the pastor to be out-of-role, but because of restrictions of time and opportunity, these relationships are few and do not always provided as much time as the pastor needs. Thus, we came to a final series of recommendations that pastors develop an intentional strategy for reaching out to form new friendships, understand the dynamics of their current friendships, and incorporate those a wide range of friendships as part of a meaningful self-care strategy.

My fear, however, is that the technicalities of this project may have left us with a feeling that friendships are quite very earthy and operative relationships; that friendship has an essentially functional role that when applied correctly produces good outcomes; and that friendship is a relationship to be administered strategically as a part of good life management. Knowing that analysis can gradually place a cold distance between us and our subject, I want to invite the mysteries of this relationship back into their proper place.

As people of faith, we recognize that earthy things are fundamentally spiritual in nature, and so is friendship. Friendship tends not only to the many practical needs within the human being, but there is something transcendent about friendship that makes it a holy experience. Embedded in the Trinity itself is the essential fact that God as a divine being relates within His own being as Father, Son, and Spirit. Relational connectedness is more than just good practice. It is at the heart of what it means to exist. It is a fundamental nature within God and is a fundamental part of who we are. To share in friendship, then, is to share in something basic about ourselves, about who God is, and about the way God made the world. It is not a relationship that evolved out of humankind's need. It was gifted to us long before there ever was "need." It exists for its own sake. It was woven in the fabric of existence long before the Fall and is a foreshadowing of the relational completion we will experience in the kingdom life to come.

We heard at times throughout our study from the Theological Colloquium at Duke Divinity School. This group came to describe friendships as "holy friendships." "What sets them apart is that they have a larger purpose beyond the friendship itself: they help point us towards God."[75] They describe friendship as "rooted in the very nature of church and the Christian story."[76] The group came to realize that pastors held an impoverished few of friendship. The pastors they spoke with described friendship to be somewhat banal and much less spiritual than other relationships in their lives. Given the limits of their time, pastors would choose more substantive relationships, the kind that might shape and form them spiritually.

Paul Wadell argues that friendship does exactly that. In *Friendship and the Moral Life*, he speaks to the highly formative nature of friendship and advocates for its spiritual essence. Friendship at its best, he says, enables two people to help one another become the good they desire to be.[77] For it is in friendship that two people seek together to be the best of themselves. "We cannot be good without them," Wadell argues.[78] Many have considered friendship to be a self-serving relationship because people seek out others who share things in common. Wadell says that what we are doing in friendship is seeking out others who share our goals,

---

[75] Wells, "Friendship: It's Okay to Go There," 8.

[76] Wells, "Friendship: It's Okay to Go There," 4.

[77] Paul J. Wadell, *Friendship and the Moral Life* (Notre Dame: University of Notre Dame Press, 1989), 6.

[78] Wadell, *Friendship and the Moral Life*, 6.

common interests, and concerns, because our spiritual development requires "the ongoing presence of another who shares that good."[79]

When pastors seek good friendships, they are seeking out others who will journey with them in their faith development. Friendship, then, is doing so much more than helping the pastor cope with stress or escape his role or delight in recreation. Friendship shapes the moral and spiritual fabric of the pastor's life. Friendship helps the pastor move beyond the theological and ethereal world of spiritual reflection to the gritty world of spiritual practice. The spiritual life is what happens when we are in relationship to others. A friend is not a person completely apart from us, but is a "second-self" sharing the struggle of life and growth with us.[80] Friends are our spiritual co-creators.

That spiritual formation is connected to friendship is never more evident than in the biblical invitation to become a "friend of God." While that was initially a descriptor from God to Abraham,[81] we know that Jesus too came to call his followers his friends.[82] What began with Abraham has been extended to all who follow Jesus Christ. To be in relationship with Christ is to be invited into the place of closest intimacy with God as His friend. To be God's friend is to hear God say that in true relationship with Him, the power-distance between God and his followers has been effectively removed through His divine grace. Every time we relate to one another in friendship, we are pointed to our friendship with God. Friendship itself can be a source of worship, wonder, and awe for the believer. For earthly friendship is but a dim shadow of the grand friendship we have with God.

Friendship, then, in light of the Christian story, is a God-given relationship aimed at shaping us for relationship with Him. Unlike Kierkegaard who struggled to see beyond the self-beneficial functions of friendship, we can delight in what friendship reveals to us about God and how it shapes us to become more like Christ. Friendship fosters interdependence and submission for the sake of the other, critical components of the faith relationship. As we learn interdependence with a friend, we grow in our capacity to be interdependent with God.

This may ultimately be the reason pastors ought to seek out and nourish good friendships. These relationships, more than any other, shape us to be not only the best pastor we can be, but the best person we can be. Pastors are held to high standards, but the reality is that pastors struggle too on their journey of faith. The true friend can enter the

---

[79] Wadell, *Friendship and the Moral Life*, 6.
[80] Wadell, *Friendship and the Moral Life*, 142.
[81] James 2:23.
[82] John 15:15.

pastor's life not simply to commiserate with the pastor's struggles, but help the pastor rise out where he or she is into something more like Christ. As Dan, one of the pastors in our study, said, "A true friend is not only loyal, not only dedicated, but they want to make you more like Jesus."[83]

It may be said then that of all the loving and well-meaning people in the pastor's life, the pastor's close friend is one of the most essential. It was true for King David. David fought fear and doubt and intrigue in those early days of his call. Perhaps he wondered if God's plan for him would ever come to pass. Likely, it would not have without the personal devotion of his soulmate, Jonathan. Jonathan came to bear the hope that David required. Jonathan's sacrifice and loyalty sustained David through the most frightening of times. Jonathan inspired in David the best of himself. And ultimately, when a desperate King David feared for his very life, Jonathan made this promise: "You shall be king over Israel, and I shall be next to you."[84]

Blessed is the pastor who has next to him a friend.

---

[83] "Dan," Interview with author, November 18, 2013.
[84] I Samuel 23:17 (ESV).

Bibliography

Adams, Rebecca, and Graham Allan, eds. *Placing Friendships in Context*. Cambridge: Cambridge University Press, 1998.

Aristotle. *Nicomachean Ethics*. Library of Constitutional Classics, n.d. Accessed January 19, 2014. http://www.constitution.org/ari/ethic_08.htm.

————. *The Nicomachean Ethics of Aristotle*. London: George Bell and Sons, 1889.

Badhwar, Neera Kapur, ed. *Friendship: A Philosophical Reader*. Ithaca, NY: Cornell University Press, 1993.

"Barely Half of Weekly Churchgoers Think Pastors Contribute 'A Lot' to Society." *Gleanings-Important Developments in the Church and the World*. Accessed July 21, 2013. http://www.christianitytoday.com/gleanings/2013/july/pew-half-weekly-churchgoers-esteem-pastors.html.

Barna, George. *Today's Pastors*. Ventura, CA: Regal Books, 1993.

Bell, Robert. *Worlds of Friendship*. Beverly Hills, CA: Sage Publications, 1981.

Benware, Paul N. *Understanding End Times Prophecy: A Comprehensive Approach*. Chicago: Moody Press, 1995.

Berryman, Jerome. *Godly Play: An Imaginative Approach to Religious Education*. Minneapolis, MN: Augsburg Books, 1994.

Blieszner, Rosemary, and Rebecca G Adams. *Adult Friendship*. Newbury Park, CA: Sage Publications, 1992.

Blosser, Philip, and Marshell Carl Bradley, eds. *Friendship: Philosophic Reflections on a Perennial Concern*. Lanham, MD: University Press of America, 1997.

Brueggemann, Walter. *First and Second Samuel*. Louisville, KY: John Knox Press, 2012.

Caine, Barbara, ed. *Friendship: A History*. London: Equinox Publishing, 2009.

Carmichael, Liz. *Friendship: Interpreting Christian Love*. London: T&T Clark International, 2004.

Chandler, Charles H. "Five Relationships Every Minister Needs to Develop." *Ministering to Ministers Foundation, Inc.*, 2010. Accessed January 11, 2011. http://mtmfoundation.org/files/Five%20Relationships%20Every%20Minister%20Needs%20to%20Develop.pdf.

Cooper, John M. *Reason and Emotion: Essays on Ancient Moral Psychology and Ethical Theory*. Princeton, NJ: Princeton University Press, 1999.

Degges-White, Suzanne, and Christine Borzumato-Gainey. *Friends Forever: How Girls and Women Forge Lasting Relationships*. Lanham, MD: Rowman & Littlefield Publishers, 2011.

Dobson, James, and Gary Bauer. *Children at Risk*. Dallas: Word Publishing, 1990.

Duck, Steve. *Friends, For Life: The Psychology of Personal Relationships*. 2nd ed. New York: Harvester Wheatsheaf, 1991.

Emerson, Ralph Waldo. *Collected Essays: The Complete Original First Series*. Rockville MD: Arc Manor, 2007.

Fehr, Beverley. *Friendship Processes*. Thousand Oaks, CA: Sage Publications, 1996.

Gerig, Bruce. "Jonathan and David: An Introduction." *The Epistle*, 2005. Accessed January 17, 2014. http://epistle.us/hbarticles/jondave1.html.

Goodstein, Laurie. "Disowning Conservative Politics, Evangelical Pastor Rattles Flock." *New York Times*. Accessed December 2, 2010. http://www.nytimes.com/2006/07/30/ us/30pastor.html.

Greif, Geoffrey L. *Buddy System: Understanding Male Friendships*. Oxford: Oxford University Press, 2009.

Grenz, Stanley J. *A Primer on Postmodernism*. Grand Rapids: William B. Eerdmans, 1996.

Griffin, Emory. "Self-Disclosure: How Far Should A Leader Go?" *Leadership* 1, no. 2 (Spring 1980): 125–132.

Guder, Darrell, and Lois Barrett. *Missional Church: A Vision for the Sending of the Church in North America*. Grand Rapids: William B. Eerdmans, 1998.

Hatcher, S. Wayne, and Joe Ray Underwood. "Self-Concept and Stress: A Study of a Group of Southern Baptist Ministers." *Counseling and Values* 34, no. 3 (April 1990): 187–196.

Healy, Mary. "Civic Friendship." *Studies in Philosophy and Education* 30, no. 3 (May 1, 2011): 229–240.

Hunsberger, George, and Craig Van Gelder. *The Church Between Gospel and Culture : The Emerging Mission in North America*. Grand Rapids: William B. Eerdmans, 1996.

Irvine, Andrew R. *Between Two Worlds: Understanding and Managing Clergy Stress*. London: Mowbray, 1997.

Jelen, Ted G. *Sacred Markets, Sacred Canopies: Essays on Religious Markets and Religious Pluralism*. Lanham, MD: Rowman & Littlefield Publishers, 2002.

Kavanaugh, James. *Will You Be My Friend?* Highland Park, IL: Steven J Nash Pub, 1991.

Konstan, David. *Friendship in the Classical World*. Cambridge: Cambridge University Press, 1996.

Lewis, C. S. *The Four Loves*. New York: Harcourt Brace Jovanovich, 1991.

London, H. B., and Neil B. Wiseman. *Pastors at Greater Risk*. Ventura, CA: Gospel Light, 2003.

Malakh-Pines, Ayala, Elliot Aronson, and Ditsa Kafry. *Burnout : From Tedium to Personal Growth*. New York: Free Press, 1981.

Marsden, George. *Understanding Fundamentalism and Evangelicalism*. Grand Rapids: William B. Eerdmans, 1991.

Maslach, Christina. *Burnout : The Cost of Caring*. Englewood Cliffs, NJ: Prentice-Hall, 1982.

McCall, George J. *Friendship as a Social Institution*. New Brunswick, NJ: Transaction Publishers, 2011.

McNeal, Reggie. *The Present Future: Six Tough Questions for the Church*. San Francisco: Jossey-Bass, 2003.

Miner, Maureen, Sam Sterland, and Martin Dowson. "Coping with Ministry: Development of a Multidimensional Measure of Internal

Orientation to the Demands of Ministry." *Review of Religious Research* 48, no. 2 (2006): 212–230.

———. "Orientation to the Demands of Ministry: Construct Validity and Relationship with Burnout." *Review of Religious Research* 50, no. 4 (June 1, 2009): 463–479.

Moltmann, Jürgen. "Open Friendship: Aristotelian and Christian Concepts of Friendship." In *The Changing Face of Friendship*, edited by Leroy S. Rouner. Vol. 15. Boston University Studies in Philosphy and Religion. Notre Dame: University of Notre Dame Press, 1994.

Moltmann, Jürgen, and M. Douglas Meeks. *The Open Church: Invitation to a Messianic Lifestyle.* London: SCM Press, 1978.

Moltmann-Wendel, Elisabeth. *Rediscovering Friendship: Awakening to the Power and Promise of Women's Friendships.* Minneapolis: Fortress Press, 2001.

O'Day, Gail R. "Jesus as Friend in the Gospel of John." *Interpretation* 58, no. 2 (April 2004): 144–157.

Olds, Jacqueline, and Richard Schwartz. *The Lonely American: Drifting Apart in the Twenty-First Century.* Boston: Beacon Press, 2009.

Oswald, Roy M. *Clergy Self-Care: Finding a Balance For Effective Ministry.* Washington, DC: Alban Institute, 1991.

Pahl, Ray. *On Friendship.* Malden, MA: Polity Press, 2000.

Pakaluk, Michael, ed. *Other Selves: Philosophers on Friendship.* Indianapolis: Hackett Pub. Co., 1991.

"Pastoral Ministries 2009 Survey," Focus on the Family, 2009. Accessed January 17, 2014. http://fergusonconsultinggroup.com/images/Pastoral_Survey_2009.pdf.

Pew Forum on Religion and Public Life. "Many Americans Mix Multiple Faith." Washington, DC: Pew Research Center, December 2009. Accessed January 10, 2011. http://www.pewforum.org/files/2009/12/multiplefaiths.pdf.

"Pulpit and Pew National Survey of Pastoral Leaders." Pulpit & Pew, 2001. Accessed March 17, 2013. http://www.thearda.com/Archive/Files/0043odebooks/CLERGY01_CB.asp.

Rawlins, William K. *Friendship Matters: Communication, Dialectics, and the Life Course.* New York: Aldine de Gruyter, 1992.

————. *The Compass of Friendship: Narratives, Identities, and Dialogues*. Los Angeles: Sage Publications, 2009.

Rediger, G. Lloyd. *Clergy Killers: Guidance for Pastors and Congregations Under Attack*. Louisville, KY: Westminster John Knox Press, 1997.

Reed, Bruce D. *The Dynamics of Religion: Process and Movement in Christian Churches*. London: Darton, Longman and Todd, 1978.

Reinders, Hans S. *Receiving the Gift of Friendship: Profound Disability, Theological Anthropology, and Ethics*. Grand Rapids: William B. Eerdmans, 2008.

Reohr, Janet. *Friendship: An Exploration of Structure and Process*. New York: Garland Publishing, Inc., 1991.

Rubin, Lillian B. *Just Friends: The Role of Friendship in Our Lives*. New York: Harper & Row, 1985.

Ruf, Henry. *Postmodern Rationality, Social Criticism, and Religion*. St. Paul, MN: Paragon House, 2005.

Schoun, Benjamin D. "Can a Pastor Have Friends?" *Ministry: International Journal for Clergy*, July 1986, 8–10.

Scott, John, and Gordon Marshall. *A Dictionary of Sociology*. Oxford: Oxford University Press, 2005.

Shalev, Meir. *The First and Second Books of Samuel*. Edinburg: Canongate Books, 1999.

Spencer, Liz, and Ray Pahl. *Rethinking Friendship: Hidden Solidarities Today*. Princeton, NJ: Princeton University Press, 2006.

Stott, John R. W. *The Message of Acts: The Spirit, the Church & the World*. The Bible Speaks Today. Downers Grove, IL: Inter-Varsity Press, 1994.

Twitchell, James B. *Shopping for God: How Christianity Went From in Your Heart to in Your Face*. New York: Simon & Schuster, 2007.

Valk, Frank Vander. "Friendship, Politics, and Augustine's Consolidation of the Self." *Relig. Stud. Religious Studies* 45, no. 2 (2009): 125–146.

Vernon, Mark. *The Meaning of Friendship*. New York: Palgrave Macmillan, 2010.

Wadell, Paul J. *Becoming Friends: Worship, Justice, and the Practice of Christian Friendship*. Grand Rapids: Brazos Press, 2002.

Wadell, Paul J. *Friendship and the Moral Life*. Notre Dame: University of Notre Dame Press, 1989.

Wells, Bob. "Friendship: It's Okay to Go There." *Divinity* 2, no. 2 (Winter 2003): 4–8.

Werking, Kathy. *We're Just Good Friends: Women and Men in Nonromantic Relationships*. New York: Guilford Press, 1997.

White, Carolinne. *Christian Friendship in the Fourth Century*. Cambridge: Cambridge University Press, 2002.

Wilson, Michael Todd, and Brad Hoffmann. *Preventing Ministry Failure*. Downers Grove, IL: InterVarsity Press, 2007.

Winstead, Barbara A., Valerian J. Derlega, and Suzanna Rose. *Gender and Close Relationships*. Thousand Oaks, CA: Sage Publications, 1997.

Woods, Tim. *Beginning Postmodernism*. Manchester: Manchester University Press, 1999.

About the Author

 David Bryan Simmons was born on November 15, 1971, in Dallas, Texas. David is a graduate of Liberty University in Lynchburg, Virginia, where he attained a Bachelors of Science Degree in Secondary English Education. Though certified to teach secondary English, David experienced a call to ministry and entered seminary in pursuit of his Masters of Divinity. David graduated with his M.Div. with Biblical Languages from Southwestern Baptist Theological Seminary in Fort Worth, Texas in 1996.

David served in several areas of congregational ministry before serving a six year pastorate at Temple Baptist Church in Newport News, Virginia. Then, in 2006, David relocated to Harrisburg, Pennsylvania, where he served six years as pastor of Locust Lane (Mennonite) Chapel in Harrisburg, PA. During this time, David pursued his Doctor of Ministry degree at Gordon Conwell Theological Seminary in South Hamilton, Massachusetts, where he graduated in May, 2014, with his Doctor of Ministry Degree.

After 20 years of congregational ministry, David began a transition into hospital chaplaincy. In 2011, David entered Clinical Pastoral Education Residency at the Penn State Milton S. Hershey Medical Center in Hershey, Pennsylvania, where upon completion he was called to the position of Palliative Care and Trauma Chaplain, which he currently serves. As part of the Palliative Care team, he comes alongside patients and families facing critical illness and end-of-life issues. David's work with trauma services includes coordinating the work of the pastoral care department to provide 24/7 pastoral care to victims of trauma.

David is ordained a Southern Baptist minister and is endorsed for chaplaincy through the Cooperative Baptist Fellowship.

He is married to Tara Prowant Simmons. They have three children, Connor, Alex, and Lillie.